DOWN HOME

Delicious

CLASSIC SOUTHERN FAVORITES FOR FAMILIES AND FRIENDS

pil

Publications International, Ltd.

Artwork throughout and photograph on front cover and page 113 © Shutterstock.com

Pictured on the front cover: Buttermilk Fried Chicken *(page 112).*

Pictured on the back cover *(top to bottom):* Old-Fashioned Chicken and Dumplings *(page 116),* Cherry Soda Poke Cake *(page 161)* and Deep Bayou Chowder *(page 59).*

ISBN: 978-1-63938-457-0

Manufactured in China.

8 7 6 5 4 3 2 1

Microwave Cooking: Microwave ovens vary in wattage. Use the cooking times as guidelines and check for doneness before adding more time.

Let's get social!
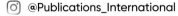 @Publications_International
@PublicationsInternational
www.pilbooks.com

Contents

Breakfast Anytime

BACON-CHEESE GRITS

2 cups milk

½ cup quick-cooking grits

1½ cups (6 ounces) shredded sharp Cheddar cheese

2 tablespoons butter

1 teaspoon Worcestershire sauce

½ teaspoon salt

⅛ teaspoon ground red pepper (optional)

4 slices thick-cut bacon, crisp-cooked and chopped

1. Bring milk to a boil in large saucepan over medium-high heat. Slowly stir in grits; return to a boil. Reduce heat to low; cover and simmer 5 minutes, stirring frequently.

2. Remove from heat; stir in cheese, butter, Worcestershire sauce, salt and red pepper, if desired. Cover and let stand 2 minutes or until cheese is melted. Top with bacon.

Makes 4 servings

TIP: For a thinner consistency, add an additional ½ cup milk.

Breakfast Anytime

LOADED BANANA BREAD

1½	cups all-purpose flour	3	ripe bananas, mashed
2½	teaspoons baking powder	½	teaspoon vanilla
¼	teaspoon salt	1	can (8 ounces) crushed pineapple, drained
6	tablespoons (¾ stick) butter, softened	⅓	cup flaked coconut
⅓	cup granulated sugar	¼	cup mini chocolate chips
⅓	cup packed brown sugar	⅓	cup chopped walnuts (optional)
2	eggs		

1. Preheat oven to 350°F. Spray 9×5-inch loaf pan with nonstick cooking spray.

2. Combine flour, baking powder and salt in small bowl; mix well. Beat butter, granulated sugar and brown sugar in large bowl with electric mixer at medium speed about 3 minutes or until light and fluffy. Beat in eggs, one at a time, scraping down bowl after each addition. Add bananas and vanilla; beat just until blended.

3. Slowly add flour mixture; beat just until blended. Fold in pineapple, coconut and chocolate chips. Spread batter in prepared pan; top with walnuts, if desired.

4. Bake 50 minutes or until toothpick inserted into center comes out clean. Cool in pan 1 hour; remove to wire rack to cool completely.

Makes 1 loaf

OATMEAL PECAN PANCAKES

1¼ to 1½ cups milk, divided

½ cup old-fashioned oats

⅔ cup all-purpose flour

⅓ cup whole wheat flour

2½ tablespoons packed
     brown sugar

2 teaspoons baking powder

½ teaspoon baking soda

¼ teaspoon salt

1 egg

2 tablespoons butter,
     melted, plus additional
     for serving

½ cup chopped toasted pecans
     (see Tip)

Maple syrup

1. Bring ½ cup milk to a simmer in small saucepan; stir in oats. Remove from heat; let stand 10 minutes.

2. Combine all-purpose flour, whole wheat flour, brown sugar, baking powder, baking soda and salt in large bowl; mix well.

3. Beat egg and 2 tablespoons melted butter in medium bowl; mix well. Stir in oatmeal and ¾ cup milk. Add to flour mixture; stir just until blended. *Do not beat.* If batter is too thick, thin with remaining ¼ cup milk, 1 tablespoon at a time. Stir in pecans.

4. Lightly grease large skillet or griddle; heat over medium heat. Pour batter into skillet by ¼ cupfuls; flatten slightly. Cook 2 minutes or until tops are bubbly and bottoms are golden brown. Turn and cook 2 minutes or until golden brown. Serve with maple syrup and additional butter.

Makes 4 servings

TIP: To toast pecans, cook in small skillet over medium heat 1 to 2 minutes or until lightly browned, stirring frequently. Cool before using.

APPLE-SAGE BREAKFAST SAUSAGE

1 pound ground pork	1 teaspoon minced garlic
¼ cup applesauce	1 teaspoon minced fresh sage
1 tablespoon maple syrup	½ teaspoon black pepper
1½ teaspoons salt	¼ teaspoon ground nutmeg

1. Preheat classic waffle maker to medium-high heat.

2. Combine pork, applesauce, maple syrup, salt, garlic, sage, pepper and nutmeg in large bowl; mix well.

3. Roll ¼ cupfuls of pork mixture into balls with hands, making six to eight balls total. Place on large plate; slightly flatten balls into patties.

4. Working in batches, place patties on waffle maker; close lightly. Cook about 3 minutes or until dark brown waffle marks appear and sausages are cooked through. Remove to plate; tent with foil to keep warm. Wipe grids of waffle maker with paper towels between batches as needed to absorb excess fat.

Makes 3 to 4 servings

Breakfast Anytime

RASPBERRY CORN MUFFINS

1 cup all-purpose flour

¾ cup yellow cornmeal

½ cup sugar

2 teaspoons baking powder

½ teaspoon baking soda

½ teaspoon salt

⅔ cup sour cream

⅓ cup milk

¼ cup (½ stick) butter, melted

1 egg

1¼ cups fresh or frozen raspberries

1. Preheat oven to 400°F. Spray 12 standard (2½-inch) muffin cups with nonstick cooking spray or line with paper baking cups.

2. Combine flour, cornmeal, sugar, baking powder, baking soda and salt in large bowl; mix well. Whisk sour cream, milk, butter and egg in medium bowl until well blended. Add to flour mixture; stir just until combined. *Do not overmix.* Gently fold in raspberries. Spoon batter evenly into prepared muffin cups.

3. Bake 16 to 18 minutes or until toothpick inserted into centers comes out clean. Cool in pan 5 minutes; remove to wire rack to cool completely.

Makes 12 muffins

HAM AND CHEESE BREAD PUDDING

1 small loaf (8 ounces) sourdough, country French or Italian bread, sliced

3 tablespoons butter, softened

8 ounces ham or smoked ham, cubed

1 cup (4 ounces) shredded Cheddar cheese

3 eggs

2 cups milk

1 teaspoon ground mustard

½ teaspoon salt

⅛ teaspoon white pepper

1. Spray 11×7-inch baking dish with nonstick cooking spray. Spread one side of each bread slice with butter. Cut bread into 1-inch cubes; place in prepared baking dish. Top with ham; sprinkle with cheese.

2. Beat eggs in medium bowl. Whisk in milk, mustard, salt and pepper until blended. Pour egg mixture evenly over bread mixture; cover and refrigerate at least 6 hours or overnight.

3. Preheat oven to 350°F. Bake bread pudding, uncovered, 45 to 50 minutes or until puffed and golden brown and knife inserted into center comes out clean. Serve immediately.

Makes 8 servings

MAPLE BACON MONKEY BREAD

10	slices bacon, cooked and coarsely chopped (about 12 ounces)	3	tablespoons butter
		3	tablespoons maple syrup
⅓	cup packed brown sugar	1	loaf (16 ounces) frozen bread dough, thawed according to package directions
¼	teaspoon black pepper		

1. Spray 12-cup (10-inch) bundt pan with nonstick cooking spray.

2. Combine bacon, brown sugar and pepper in large bowl; mix well. Combine butter and maple syrup in medium microwavable bowl; microwave on HIGH 30 seconds. Stir; microwave 20 seconds or until butter is melted.

3. Roll 1-inch pieces of dough into balls. Dip balls in butter mixture; roll in bacon mixture to coat. Layer in prepared pan. Reheat any remaining butter mixture, if necessary; drizzle over top of dough. Cover and let rise in warm place about 45 minutes or until doubled in size. Preheat oven to 350°F.

4. Bake 30 to 35 minutes or until golden brown. Cool in pan on wire rack 5 minutes. Loosen edge of bread with knife; invert onto serving plate. Serve warm.

Makes 12 servings

CHICKEN AND WAFFLES WITH SRIRACHA MAPLE SYRUP

Chicken

½ cup milk

1 egg

1¼ pounds chicken tenderloins (about 8 pieces)

1½ cups panko bread crumbs

1 teaspoon salt

1 teaspoon garlic powder

1 teaspoon paprika

½ teaspoon black pepper

¼ cup vegetable oil

Waffles

2 cups pancake and baking mix

1⅓ cups milk

1 egg

Sriracha Maple Syrup

½ cup pure maple syrup

2 teaspoons sriracha sauce

1. Whisk ½ cup milk and 1 egg in medium bowl until blended. Add chicken; stir to coat.

2. Combine panko, salt, garlic powder, paprika and pepper in shallow pie plate or dish. Working with one piece at a time, coat chicken with panko mixture, pressing down lightly to adhere. Remove to plate.

3. Heat oil in large skillet over medium-high heat. Reduce heat to medium; cook chicken about 6 minutes per side or until golden brown and no longer pink in center. Remove to clean plate; tent with foil to keep warm.

4. Preheat waffle maker to medium; spray with nonstick cooking spray. Combine baking mix, milk and egg in medium bowl; mix well. Pour ¾ cup batter into waffle maker; cook 3 to 4 minutes or until golden brown. Remove to serving plate. Repeat with remaining batter.

5. Combine maple syrup and sriracha in small bowl; mix well. Serve waffles topped with chicken; drizzle with syrup.

Makes 4 to 6 servings

TIP: If desired, drizzle each waffle with 1 tablespoon melted butter before topping with chicken and syrup.

HAM AND SWISS CHEESE BISCUITS

2 cups all-purpose flour

2 teaspoons baking powder

$\frac{1}{2}$ teaspoon baking soda

$\frac{1}{4}$ teaspoon salt

$\frac{1}{2}$ cup (1 stick) cold butter, cut into small pieces

$\frac{2}{3}$ cup buttermilk

$\frac{1}{2}$ cup (2 ounces) shredded Swiss cheese

2 ounces ham, finely chopped

1. Preheat oven to 450°F. Line baking sheet with parchment paper or spray with nonstick cooking spray.

2. Combine flour, baking powder, baking soda and salt in medium bowl; mix well. Cut in butter with pastry blender or two knives until mixture resembles coarse crumbs. Stir in buttermilk, 1 tablespoon at a time, until slightly sticky dough forms. Stir in cheese and ham.

3. Turn out dough onto lightly floured surface; knead lightly. Roll out dough to ½-inch thickness. Cut out biscuits with 2-inch round cutter; place on prepared baking sheet.

4. Bake 10 minutes or until browned. Serve warm.

Makes about 18 biscuits

CARAMELIZED BACON

12 slices (about 12 ounces) applewood-smoked bacon	2 tablespoons water
$\frac{1}{2}$ cup packed brown sugar	$\frac{1}{4}$ to $\frac{1}{2}$ teaspoon ground red pepper

1. Preheat oven to 375°F. Line 15×10-inch rimmed baking sheet with foil. Spray wire rack with nonstick cooking spray; place on prepared baking sheet.

2. Arrange bacon in single layer on prepared wire rack. Combine brown sugar, water and red pepper in small bowl; mix well. Brush mixture generously over bacon.

3. Bake 20 to 25 minutes or until bacon is well browned. Immediately remove to serving platter; cool completely.

Makes 6 servings

NOTE: The bacon can be prepared up to 3 days ahead and stored in the refrigerator between sheets of waxed paper in a resealable food storage bag. Let stand at room temperature at least 30 minutes before serving.

HEARTY HASH BROWN CASSEROLE

2 cups sour cream

2 cups (8 ounces) shredded Colby cheese, divided

1 can (10¾ ounces) cream of chicken soup

½ cup (1 stick) butter, melted

1 small onion, finely chopped

¾ teaspoon salt

½ teaspoon black pepper

1 package (30 ounces) frozen shredded hash brown potatoes, thawed

1. Preheat oven to 375°F. Spray 13×9-inch baking dish with nonstick cooking spray.

2. Combine sour cream, 1½ cups cheese, soup, butter, onion, salt and pepper in large bowl; mix well. Add potatoes; stir until well blended. Spread mixture in prepared baking dish. (Do not pack down.) Sprinkle with remaining ½ cup cheese.

3. Bake 45 minutes or until cheese is melted and top of casserole is beginning to brown.

Makes about 16 servings

APPLE BUTTER SPICE MUFFINS

½ cup sugar

1 teaspoon ground cinnamon

¼ teaspoon ground nutmeg

⅛ teaspoon ground allspice

½ cup chopped pecans or walnuts

2 cups all-purpose flour

2 teaspoons baking powder

¼ teaspoon salt

1 cup milk

¼ cup vegetable oil

1 egg

¼ cup apple butter

1. Preheat oven to 400°F. Line 12 standard (2½-inch) muffin cups with paper baking cups or spray with nonstick cooking spray.

2. Combine sugar, cinnamon, nutmeg and allspice in large bowl; mix well. Remove 2 tablespoons sugar mixture to small bowl; toss with pecans until coated. Add flour, baking powder and salt to remaining sugar mixture.

3. Whisk milk, oil and egg in medium bowl until well blended. Add to flour mixture; stir just until dry ingredients are moistened. Spoon 1 tablespoon batter into each prepared muffin cup. Top with 1 teaspoon apple butter; spoon remaining batter evenly over apple butter. Sprinkle with pecan mixture.

4. Bake 20 to 25 minutes or until golden brown and toothpick inserted into centers comes out clean. Remove to wire rack to cool 10 minutes. Serve warm or cool completely.

Makes 12 muffins

Breakfast Anytime

SWEET POTATO BREAKFAST NESTS

1 sweet potato (12 to 16 ounces)

1 teaspoon vegetable oil

¼ teaspoon salt

¼ teaspoon ground nutmeg

¼ teaspoon black pepper

4 eggs

1. Preheat oven to 375°F. Line four 6- to 8-ounce ramekins with squares of parchment paper; spray parchment with nonstick cooking spray. Place ramekins on baking sheet.

2. Spiral sweet potatoes with thin ribbon blade.* Loosely pile on cutting board and cut in an X. Place in medium bowl. Add oil, salt, nutmeg and pepper; toss to coat. Arrange sweet potatoes evenly in nests in prepared ramekins.

3. Bake 20 minutes. Remove from oven. Carefully press down sweet potatoes with spatula. Crack one egg over sweet potatoes in each ramekin. Bake 15 minutes or until whites are set and yolks are desired doneness. Remove from ramekins using parchment.

If you don't have a spiralizer, use julienne peeler to cut sweet potatoes or cut into julienne strips with sharp knife.

Makes 4 servings

Appetizers & Snacks

PIMIENTO CHEESE

½ (8-ounce) package cream cheese, softened

½ cup mayonnaise

2 cups (8 ounces) shredded Cheddar cheese

½ cup chopped drained pimientos (about 4 ounces)

⅓ cup finely chopped pimiento-stuffed green olives

⅓ cup finely chopped green onions

1 teaspoon garlic powder

1 teaspoon paprika

Toasted bread slices and/or assorted crackers

1. Beat cream cheese and mayonnaise in medium bowl until well blended and smooth.

2. Stir in Cheddar, pimientos, olives, green onions, garlic powder and paprika; mix well. Serve with bread and/or crackers.

Makes about 2½ cups

FRIED GREEN TOMATOES

1/3 cup all-purpose flour

1/4 teaspoon salt

2 eggs

1 tablespoon water

1/2 cup panko bread crumbs

2 large green tomatoes, cut into 1/2-inch-thick slices

1/2 cup olive oil

1/2 cup ranch dressing

1 tablespoon sriracha sauce

1 package (5 ounces) spring greens salad mix

1/4 cup crumbled goat cheese

1. Combine flour and salt in shallow bowl. Beat eggs and water in another shallow bowl. Place panko in third shallow bowl. Coat both sides of tomato slices with flour mixture, shaking off excess. Dip in egg mixture, letting excess drip back into bowl. Roll in panko to coat. Place on plate.

2. Heat oil in large skillet over medium-high heat. Add half of tomato slices, arranging in single layer in skillet. (Cook in two batches as necessary; do not overlap in skillet.) Cook about 2 minutes per side or until golden brown. Remove to paper towel-lined plate.

3. Combine ranch dressing and sriracha in small bowl; mix well. Divide greens among four serving plates; top with tomatoes. Drizzle with dressing mixture; sprinkle with cheese.

Makes 4 servings

CLASSIC DEVILED EGGS

6 eggs

3 tablespoons mayonnaise

1 tablespoon minced fresh dill *or* 1 teaspoon dried dill weed

1 tablespoon minced dill pickle (optional)

1 teaspoon Dijon mustard

¼ teaspoon salt

⅛ teaspoon white pepper

Paprika (optional)

Fresh dill sprigs (optional)

1. Bring medium saucepan of water to a boil. Gently add eggs with slotted spoon. Reduce heat to maintain a simmer; cook 12 minutes.

2. Meanwhile, fill medium bowl with cold water and ice cubes. Drain eggs and place in ice water; cool 10 minutes.

3. Peel eggs. Cut eggs in half; place yolks in small bowl. Add mayonnaise, minced dill, pickle, if desired, mustard, salt and pepper; mash with fork until well blended.

4. Fill egg halves with yolk mixture using teaspoon or piping bag fitted with large plain tip. Garnish with paprika and dill sprigs.

Makes 6 servings

CRAB SHACK DIP

½ (8-ounce) package cream cheese, softened

½ cup sour cream

2 tablespoons mayonnaise

¾ teaspoon seasoned salt

¼ teaspoon paprika, plus additional for garnish

2 cans (6 ounces each) crabmeat, drained and flaked

½ cup (2 ounces) shredded mozzarella cheese

2 tablespoons minced onion

2 tablespoons finely chopped green bell pepper*

Chopped fresh parsley (optional)

Tortilla chips

For a spicier dip, substitute 1 tablespoon minced jalapeño pepper for the bell pepper.

1. Preheat oven to 350°F.

2. Combine cream cheese, sour cream, mayonnaise, seasoned salt and ¼ teaspoon paprika in medium bowl; stir until well blended and smooth. Add crabmeat, mozzarella, onion and bell pepper; stir until blended. Spread in small (1-quart) shallow baking dish.

3. Bake 15 to 20 minutes or until bubbly and top is beginning to brown. Garnish with additional paprika and parsley; serve with tortilla chips.

Makes 6 to 8 servings (about 3½ cups)

ONION RING STACK

1 cup all-purpose flour, divided

½ cup cornmeal

1 teaspoon black pepper

½ teaspoon salt, plus additional for seasoning

¼ to ½ teaspoon ground red pepper

1 cup light-colored beer

Rémoulade Sauce (recipe follows) or ranch dressing

Vegetable oil for frying

6 tablespoons cornstarch, divided

2 large sweet onions, cut into ½-inch rings and separated

1. Combine ½ cup flour, cornmeal, black pepper, ½ teaspoon salt and red pepper in large bowl; mix well. Whisk in beer until well blended. Let batter stand 1 hour.

2. Prepare Rémoulade Sauce; refrigerate until ready to serve.

3. Heat 2 inches oil in large saucepan or Dutch oven over medium heat to 360° to 370°F; adjust heat to maintain temperature. Line large wire rack with paper towels.

4. Whisk 4 tablespoons cornstarch into batter. Combine remaining ½ cup flour and 2 tablespoons cornstarch in medium bowl. Thoroughly coat onions with flour mixture.

5. Working with one at a time, dip onion rings into batter to coat completely; carefully place in hot oil. Cook about 4 onion rings at a time 3 minutes or until golden brown, turning once. Remove to prepared wire rack; season with additional salt. Return oil to 370°F between batches. Serve immediately with Rémoulade Sauce.

Makes 4 to 6 servings (about 20 onion rings)

RÉMOULADE SAUCE: Combine 1 cup mayonnaise, 2 tablespoons coarse-grain mustard, 1 tablespoon lemon juice, 1 tablespoon sweet relish, 1 teaspoon horseradish sauce, 1 teaspoon Worcestershire sauce and ¼ teaspoon hot pepper sauce in medium bowl; mix well.

CITRUS CANDIED NUTS

1 egg white

1½ cups whole almonds

1½ cups pecan halves

1 cup powdered sugar

2 tablespoons lemon juice

2 teaspoons grated orange peel

1 teaspoon grated lemon peel

⅛ teaspoon ground nutmeg

1. Preheat oven to 300°F. Lightly grease large baking sheet or line with parchment paper.

2. Beat egg white in medium bowl with electric mixer at high speed until soft peaks form. Add almonds and pecans; stir until well coated.

3. Stir in powdered sugar, lemon juice, orange peel, lemon peel and nutmeg until nuts are evenly coated. Spread in single layer on prepared baking sheet.

4. Bake 30 minutes, stirring after 20 minutes. Turn off heat; let nuts stand in oven 15 minutes. Remove nuts to sheet of foil; cool completely. Store in airtight container up to 2 weeks.

Makes about 3 cups

CORN FRITTERS

2 large ears corn*	1/8 teaspoon black pepper
2 eggs, separated	1/8 teaspoon cream of tartar
1/4 cup all-purpose flour	1 to 2 tablespoons vegetable oil
1 tablespoon sugar	
1 tablespoon butter, melted	*The fresher the corn, the better the fritters.*
1/4 teaspoon salt	

1. Husk corn. Cut kernels from ears (1½ to 2 cups); place in medium bowl. Hold cobs over bowl; scrape cobs with back of knife to extract juice.

2. Transfer about half of kernels to food processor; process 2 to 3 seconds or until coarsely chopped. Add to whole kernels in bowl.

3. Whisk egg yolks in large bowl. Add flour, sugar, butter, salt and pepper; whisk until well blended. Stir in corn mixture.

4. Beat egg whites and cream of tartar in separate large bowl with electric mixer at high speed until stiff peaks form. Gently fold egg whites into corn mixture.

5. Heat 1 tablespoon oil in large nonstick skillet over medium-high heat. Drop batter by 1/4 cupfuls into skillet, spacing 1 inch apart. Cook 3 to 5 minutes per side or until lightly browned, adding additional oil, if necessary. Serve hot.

Makes 4 servings (8 to 9 fritters)

SPICY PICKLED RELISH

8 serrano or jalapeño peppers, thinly sliced

2 banana peppers, sliced

3 cups cauliflower florets

2 carrots, thinly sliced

½ cup salt

1½ cups olive oil

1½ cups white vinegar

3 cloves garlic, thinly sliced

1 teaspoon dried oregano

1. Layer peppers, cauliflower and carrots in large jar or large covered bowl or container. Sprinkle with salt; fill with water to cover. Cover and refrigerate overnight.

2. Drain and thoroughly rinse vegetables under cold water. Return vegetables to jar.

3. Pour oil and vinegar over vegetables. Add garlic and oregano; cover and shake or stir until well coated. Marinate in refrigerator at least 8 hours.

Makes 6 cups

SERVING SUGGESTIONS: Pickled vegetables can be served on their own as a snack, or serve them with cheese or hummus or ranch dips. Add them to crudité or antipasto platters, or use them in sandwiches, wraps and tacos.

PEACH ICED TEA

4 cups water

3 black tea bags

¼ cup sugar

1 can (about 11 ounces) peach nectar

1 cup frozen peach slices

Ice cubes

1. Bring water to a boil in medium saucepan over high heat. Remove from heat; add tea bags and let steep 5 minutes.

2. Remove tea bags; stir in sugar until dissolved. Cool to room temperature.

3. Stir in peach nectar and peach slices. Refrigerate until cold. Serve over ice.

Makes 4 servings

SOUTHERN CRAB CAKES

10 ounces fresh lump crabmeat	2 tablespoons coarse grain or spicy brown mustard, divided
1½ cups fresh white or sourdough bread crumbs, divided	¾ teaspoon hot pepper sauce, divided
¼ cup chopped green onions	2 tablespoons olive oil
½ cup mayonnaise, divided	Lemon wedges (optional)
1 egg white, lightly beaten	

1. Preheat oven to 200°F. Pick out and discard any shell or cartilage from crabmeat. Combine crabmeat, ¾ cup bread crumbs and green onions in medium bowl. Add ¼ cup mayonnaise, egg white, 1 tablespoon mustard and ½ teaspoon hot pepper sauce; mix well.

2. Shape ¼ cupfuls of crab mixture into eight ½-inch-thick cakes. Place remaining ¾ cup bread crumbs in shallow dish; roll crab cakes lightly in crumbs to coat.

3. Heat large nonstick skillet over medium heat; add 1 tablespoon oil. Add four crab cakes; cook 4 to 5 minutes per side or until golden brown. Transfer to serving platter; keep warm in oven. Repeat with remaining 1 tablespoon oil and crab cakes.

4. For sauce, combine remaining ¼ cup mayonnaise, 1 tablespoon mustard and ¼ teaspoon hot pepper sauce in small bowl; mix well.

5. Serve crab cakes warm with sauce and lemon wedges, if desired.

Makes 8 servings

JALAPEÑO POPPERS

10 to 12 jalapeño peppers*	⅛ teaspoon garlic powder
1 package (8 ounces) cream cheese, softened	6 slices bacon, crisp-cooked and finely chopped
1½ cups (6 ounces) shredded Cheddar cheese, divided	2 tablespoons grated Parmesan or Romano cheese
2 green onions, finely chopped	
½ teaspoon onion powder	*For large jalapeño poppers, use 10. For small poppers, use 12.
¼ teaspoon salt	

1. Preheat oven to 375°F. Line baking sheet with parchment paper or foil.

2. Cut each jalapeño pepper in half lengthwise; remove ribs and seeds.

3. Combine cream cheese, 1 cup Cheddar, green onions, onion powder, salt and garlic powder in medium bowl; mix well. Stir in bacon. Fill each jalapeño pepper half with about 1 tablespoon cheese mixture. Place on prepared baking sheet; sprinkle with remaining ½ cup Cheddar and Parmesan.

4. Bake 10 to 12 minutes or until cheese is melted and jalapeño peppers are slightly softened.

Makes 20 to 24 poppers

HICKORY-SMOKED BARBECUE CHICKEN WINGS

2 pounds chicken wings, tips removed, split in half

3 teaspoons hickory-flavored liquid smoke, divided

1 cup barbecue sauce

1 cup cola

⅓ cup honey

¼ cup ketchup

2 teaspoons spicy mustard

2 teaspoons hot pepper sauce

1 teaspoon Worcestershire sauce

¼ cup sliced green onions (optional)

1. Place wings in large resealable food storage bag. Add 2 teaspoons liquid smoke; seal bag and turn to coat. Refrigerate at least 1 hour.

2. Preheat oven to 375°F. Spray 13×9-inch baking pan with nonstick cooking spray.

3. Combine barbecue sauce, cola, honey, ketchup, mustard, hot pepper sauce, Worcestershire sauce and remaining 1 teaspoon liquid smoke in medium bowl; mix well. Pour sauce into prepared pan. Add wings to pan; stir to coat.

4. Bake 35 to 40 minutes or until wings are tender and no longer pink, basting occasionally with sauce and turning once.

5. Remove pan from oven and discard sauce, leaving just enough to coat wings. *Turn oven to broil.* Broil 3 to 4 minutes or until wings are browned in spots. Garnish with green onions.

Makes 24 appetizers

MAC AND CHEESE MINI CUPS

3 tablespoons butter, divided

2 tablespoons all-purpose flour

1 cup milk

1 teaspoon salt

½ teaspoon black pepper

1 cup (4 ounces) shredded sharp Cheddar cheese

1 cup (4 ounces) shredded Muenster cheese

8 ounces elbow macaroni, cooked and drained

⅓ cup panko or plain dry bread crumbs

Finely chopped fresh parsley (optional)

1. Preheat oven to 400°F. Melt 1 tablespoon butter in large saucepan over medium heat; grease 36 mini (1¾-inch) muffin cups with melted butter.

2. Melt remaining 2 tablespoons butter in same saucepan over medium heat. Whisk in flour; cook and stir 2 minutes. Add milk, salt and pepper; cook and stir 3 minutes or until thickened. Remove from heat; stir in Cheddar and Muenster cheeses. Fold in macaroni. Divide mixture evenly among prepared muffin cups; sprinkle with panko.

3. Bake about 25 minutes or until golden brown. Cool in pans 10 minutes; remove carefully using sharp knife. Garnish with parsley.

Makes 36 appetizers

PAN-FRIED OYSTERS

¼ cup all-purpose flour

½ teaspoon salt

¼ teaspoon black pepper

2 eggs

½ cup plain dry bread crumbs

5 tablespoons chopped fresh parsley, divided

2 containers (8 ounces each) shucked fresh oysters, rinsed, drained and patted dry *or* 1 pound fresh oysters, shucked and patted dry

Canola oil for frying

5 slices thick-cut bacon, crisp-cooked and chopped

Lemon wedges

1. Combine flour, salt and pepper in shallow dish or pie plate. Beat eggs in shallow bowl. Combine bread crumbs and 4 tablespoons parsley in another shallow bowl.

2. Working with one oyster at a time, coat with flour mixture, shaking off excess. Dip in eggs, shaking off excess; roll in bread crumb mixture to coat. Place coated oysters on clean plate.

3. Heat ½ inch oil in large skillet over medium-high heat until very hot but not smoking (about 370°F). Add one third of oysters; cook about 2 minutes per side or until golden brown. Drain on paper towel-lined plate. Repeat with remaining oysters.

4. Toss oysters with bacon and remaining 1 tablespoon parsley in large bowl. Serve immediately with lemon wedges.

Makes 4 appetizer servings

Soups & Salads

DEEP BAYOU CHOWDER

1 tablespoon olive oil	½ teaspoon dried thyme
1½ cups chopped onions	2 cups milk
1 large green bell pepper, chopped	2 tablespoons chopped parsley
1 large carrot, chopped	1½ teaspoons seafood seasoning
8 ounces red potatoes, diced	¾ teaspoon salt
1 cup frozen corn	
1 cup water	

1. Heat oil in large saucepan or Dutch oven over medium-high heat. Add onions, bell pepper and carrot; cook and stir 4 minutes or until onions are translucent.

2. Add potatoes, corn, water and thyme; bring to a boil over high heat. Reduce heat to medium-low; cover and simmer 15 minutes or until potatoes are tender. Stir in milk, parsley, seafood seasoning and salt; cook 5 minutes.

Makes 6 servings

STRAWBERRY SALAD

2 packages (4-serving size each) strawberry-flavored gelatin

1 cup boiling water

2 packages (10 ounces each) frozen strawberries, thawed

1 can (20 ounces) crushed pineapple, drained

2 cups sour cream

1 container (8 ounces) whipped topping, thawed

Sliced fresh strawberries and fresh mint leaves (optional)

1. Combine gelatin and boiling water in large bowl; stir until dissolved. Add frozen strawberries and pineapple; mix well.

2. Pour half of gelatin mixture into medium glass serving bowl or 13×9-inch pan. Refrigerate until soft set.

3. Spread sour cream over gelatin in bowl. Pour remaining gelatin mixture over sour cream. Refrigerate until ready to serve. Spead whipped topping over gelatin; garnish with fresh strawberries and mint.

Makes 12 to 14 servings

COUNTRY TIME MACARONI SALAD

½ cup (2 ounces) uncooked elbow macaroni

⅓ cup mayonnaise

2 teaspoons sweet pickle relish

¾ teaspoon dried dill weed

½ teaspoon salt

½ teaspoon yellow mustard

½ cup thawed frozen green peas

½ cup chopped green bell pepper

⅓ cup thinly sliced celery

4 ounces ham, cubed

⅓ cup shredded Cheddar cheese, divided

1. Cook pasta according to package directions; drain and rinse under cold water until completely cooled.

2. Meanwhile, combine mayonnaise, pickle relish, dill weed, salt and mustard in small bowl; mix well.

3. Combine peas, bell pepper, celery and ham in medium bowl.

4. Add pasta and mayonnaise mixture to pea mixture; mix well. Stir in half of cheese; sprinkle with remaining cheese. Serve immediately.

Makes 4 servings

BLACK-EYED PEA SOUP

1 large potato

2 medium onions, thinly sliced

2 carrots, thinly sliced

4 ounces bacon, diced

4 quarts water

1 pound dried black-eyed peas, rinsed and sorted

1 cup thinly sliced celery

1 meaty ham bone

1 jalapeño pepper

2 bay leaves

½ teaspoon dried thyme

Salt and black pepper

1. Peel and grate potato; place in large bowl of cold water.

2. Combine onions, carrots and bacon in large saucepan or Dutch oven; cook over medium-high heat until onions are golden brown, stirring occasionally.

3. Drain potato. Add potato, 4 quarts water, black-eyed peas, celery, ham bone, jalapeño pepper, bay leaves and thyme to onion mixture; season with salt and black pepper. Reduce heat to low; cover and simmer 3 to 4 hours. Remove and discard jalapeño pepper and bay leaves.

4. Remove ham bone to cutting board; set aside until cool enough to handle. Cut meat from bone; chop into bite-size pieces. Stir into soup.

Makes 6 to 8 servings

SWEET AND SOUR TURNIP GREEN SALAD

2 cups shredded stemmed turnip greens

2 cups torn mixed salad greens

1 cup sliced plum tomatoes or quartered cherry tomatoes

½ cup shredded carrot

⅓ cup sliced green onions

8 tablespoons water, divided

2 teaspoons all-purpose flour

1 tablespoon packed brown sugar

½ teaspoon celery seeds

Dash black pepper

1 tablespoon white wine vinegar

1. Combine turnip greens, salad greens, tomatoes and carrot in large serving bowl.

2. Combine green onions and 2 tablespoons water in small saucepan; bring to a boil over high heat. Reduce heat to medium; cover and cook 2 to 3 minutes or until green onions are tender.

3. Whisk remaining 6 tablespoons water into flour in small bowl until smooth. Stir into green onions in saucepan. Add brown sugar, celery seeds and pepper; cook and stir until mixture boils and thickens. Cook and stir 1 minute. Stir in vinegar.

4. Pour hot dressing over salad; toss to coat. Serve immediately.

Makes 4 servings

BLUE-RIBBON COLESLAW

1 medium head green cabbage, shredded

1 medium carrot, shredded

½ cup mayonnaise

½ cup milk

⅓ cup sugar

3 tablespoons lemon juice

1½ tablespoons white vinegar

½ teaspoon salt

⅛ teaspoon black pepper

1. Combine cabbage and carrot in large bowl; mix well.

2. Combine mayonnaise, milk, sugar, lemon juice, vinegar, salt and pepper in medium bowl; whisk until well blended. Add to cabbage mixture; stir until blended.

Makes 10 servings

NAVY BEAN BACON CHOWDER

1½ cups dried navy beans, rinsed and drained

2 cups cold water

6 slices thick-cut bacon

1 medium carrot, cut lengthwise into halves, then cut into 1-inch pieces

1 small turnip, cut into 1-inch pieces

1 medium onion, chopped

1 stalk celery, chopped

1 teaspoon Italian seasoning

⅛ teaspoon black pepper

1 container (48 ounces) reduced-sodium chicken broth

1 cup milk

Slow Cooker Directions

1. Soak beans overnight in cold water; drain.

2. Cook bacon in medium skillet over medium heat until almost crisp. Drain on paper towel-lined plate; crumble bacon.

3. Combine beans, bacon, carrot, turnip, onion, celery, Italian seasoning and pepper in slow cooker. Stir in broth.

4. Cover; cook on LOW 8 to 9 hours or until beans are tender. Transfer 2 cups soup mixture to food processor or blender; process until smooth. Return to slow cooker; stir in milk. Turn slow cooker to HIGH. Cover; cook 15 minutes or until heated through.

Makes 6 servings

BROCCOLI AND CAULIFLOWER SALAD

1 package (about 12 ounces) bacon, chopped	1½ cups (6 ounces) shredded Cheddar cheese
2 cups mayonnaise	1 cup chopped red onion
¼ cup sugar	1 cup dried cranberries or raisins (optional)
¼ cup white or apple cider vinegar	½ cup sunflower seeds (optional)
4 cups chopped raw broccoli	Salt and black pepper
4 cups coarsely chopped raw cauliflower	

1. Cook bacon in large skillet over medium heat until crisp. Drain on paper towel-lined plate.

2. Whisk mayonnaise, sugar and vinegar in large bowl until well blended. Stir in broccoli, cauliflower, cheese, onion and cranberries, if desired; mix well. Fold in bacon and sunflower seeds, if desired. Season with salt and pepper.

3. Serve immediately or cover and refrigerate until ready to serve.

Makes 8 servings

SWEET POTATO AND HAM SOUP

1 tablespoon butter

1 leek, thinly sliced

1 clove garlic, minced

4 cups chicken broth

2 sweet potatoes, peeled and cut into ¾-inch cubes

8 ounces ham, cut into ½-inch pieces

½ teaspoon dried thyme

¼ teaspoon salt

2 ounces stemmed spinach, coarsely chopped

1. Melt butter in large saucepan over medium heat. Add leek and garlic; cook and stir about 3 minutes or until tender.

2. Add broth, sweet potatoes, ham, thyme and salt; bring to a boil over high heat. Reduce heat to low; simmer 10 minutes or until sweet potatoes are tender.

3. Stir in spinach; cook 2 minutes or until wilted. Serve immediately.

Makes 6 servings

CREAMY FRUIT SALAD

2 jars (16 ounces each) maraschino cherries, drained

2 cans (11 ounces each) mandarin oranges, drained

1 can (20 ounces) fruit cocktail, drained

1 container (16 ounces) sour cream

1 tablespoon mayonnaise

Chopped walnuts (optional)

2 large red apples, cut into bite-size pieces

2 bananas, cut into bite-size pieces

1. Combine cherries, oranges and fruit cocktail in large serving bowl.

2. Whisk sour cream and mayonnaise in medium bowl until well blended. Add to fruit mixture; stir gently to coat. Stir in walnuts, if desired. Cover and refrigerate 2 hours.

3. Stir in apples and bananas just before serving.

Makes 8 servings

SHRIMP RÉMOULADE SALAD

12 ounces cooked shrimp, peeled and deveined (with tails on)	1½ tablespoons white wine vinegar
2 cups shredded red cabbage	1 tablespoon olive oil
2 stalks celery, finely sliced	1 tablespoon Dijon mustard
½ cup sliced green onions	2 cloves garlic, minced
3 tablespoons ketchup	¼ teaspoon salt
2 tablespoons prepared horseradish	1 package (10 ounces) frozen mustard greens or frozen spinach

1. Combine shrimp, cabbage, celery and green onions in large bowl; mix well.

2. Whisk ketchup, horseradish, vinegar, oil, mustard, garlic and salt in small bowl until well blended. Pour over shrimp mixture; toss to coat. Cover and refrigerate at least 15 minutes or up to 2 days.

3. Cook mustard greens according to package directions. Drain and cool greens; squeeze out excess water. Divide greens among serving plates or bowls; top with shrimp salad.

Makes 4 servings

RED BEAN SOUP

1 pound dried red kidney beans	2 stalks celery, chopped
2½ quarts water, divided	1 pound smoked ham hocks
1 sprig fresh thyme, plus additional for garnish	3 cloves garlic, minced
1 sprig fresh parsley	1 bay leaf
2 tablespoons butter	½ teaspoon salt
1 onion, finely chopped	¼ teaspoon black pepper
4 carrots, chopped	2 tablespoons lemon juice
	Sour cream (optional)

1. Soak beans in 1 quart water in large bowl 6 hours or overnight.

2. Drain and rinse beans. Tie together thyme and parsley sprigs with kitchen string.

3. Melt butter in large saucepan or Dutch oven over medium-high heat. Add onion; cook and stir 3 minutes or until softened. Add carrots and celery; cook and stir 5 minutes or until beginning to brown. Add remaining 1½ quarts water, beans, ham hocks, garlic, bay leaf and thyme and parsley sprigs; bring to a boil over high heat. Reduce heat to low; cover and simmer 1 hour 30 minutes or until beans are softened. Remove and discard ham hocks, thyme and parsley sprigs and bay leaf. Stir in ½ teaspoon salt and ¼ teaspoon pepper.

4. Blend soup in batches in blender or food processor until smooth. (Or use hand-held immersion blender.) Return soup to saucepan; bring to a simmer. Stir in lemon juice; season with additional salt and pepper. Serve with sour cream, if desired; garnish with additional thyme.

Makes 6 servings

BLACK BEAN SOUP: Substitute dried black beans for the red kidney beans. Proceed as directed, simmering soup 1½ to 2 hours or until beans are tender. Add 3 to 4 tablespoons dry sherry just before serving.

PEA SALAD WITH CUCUMBERS AND RED ONION

1 small seedless cucumber	2 teaspoons chopped fresh mint or oregano
½ medium red onion	½ teaspoon salt
1 red bell pepper	½ teaspoon black pepper
¼ cup mayonnaise	2 cups frozen green peas, thawed
¼ cup sour cream or Greek yogurt	
1 tablespoon lemon juice	

1. Spiral cucumber and onion with fine spiral blade. Spiral bell pepper with spiral slicing blade.* Cut vegetables into desired lengths.

2. Whisk mayonnaise, sour cream, lemon juice, mint, salt and black pepper in large serving bowl until well blended. Add peas, cucumber, onion and bell pepper; stir gently to coat.

If you don't have a spiralizer, cut vegetables into julienne strips with knife.

Makes 6 to 8 servings

Comfort Food Classics

CRISPY RANCH CHICKEN

1½ cups cornflake crumbs	1½ cups ranch salad dressing
1 teaspoon dried rosemary	3 pounds bone-in chicken pieces
½ teaspoon salt	
½ teaspoon black pepper	

1. Preheat oven to 375°F. Spray 13×9-inch baking dish with nonstick cooking spray. Combine cornflakes, rosemary, salt and pepper in medium bowl; mix well.

2. Pour salad dressing in separate medium bowl. Dip chicken pieces in dressing; turn to coat all sides. Roll chicken in crumb mixture to coat. Place in prepared baking dish.

3. Bake 50 to 55 minutes or until cooked through (165°F).

Makes 6 servings

SPICY PORK PO' BOYS

2 tablespoons chili powder

1 tablespoon salt

1 tablespoon onion powder

1 tablespoon granulated garlic

1 tablespoon paprika

1 tablespoon black pepper

1 teaspoon ground red pepper

1 pound boneless pork ribs

½ cup cola

1 tablespoon hot pepper sauce

Dash Worcestershire sauce

½ cup ketchup

4 French rolls, toasted

½ cup prepared coleslaw

1. Combine chili powder, salt, onion powder, garlic, paprika, black pepper and red pepper in small bowl; mix well. Rub mixture over pork, coating all sides. Cover and refrigerate at least 3 hours or overnight.

2. Preheat oven to 250°F. Place ribs in Dutch oven. Combine cola, hot pepper sauce and Worcestershire sauce in small bowl; drizzle over ribs.

3. Cover and bake about 4 hours or until ribs are fork-tender. Remove ribs to large bowl. Stir ketchup into Dutch oven; cook over medium heat 4 to 6 minutes or until sauce has thickened, stirring frequently.

4. Pour sauce over ribs, pulling meat apart with two forks and coating meat with sauce. Serve on rolls with coleslaw.

Makes 4 servings

SHRIMP CREOLE

2 tablespoons olive oil	2 teaspoons hot pepper sauce, or to taste
1½ cups chopped green bell peppers	1 teaspoon dried oregano
1 medium onion, chopped	¾ teaspoon salt
⅔ cup chopped celery	½ teaspoon dried thyme
2 cloves garlic, minced	¼ teaspoon black pepper
1 cup uncooked rice	1 pound medium raw shrimp, peeled and deveined (with tails on)
1 can (about 14 ounces) diced tomatoes, drained, liquid reserved	1 tablespoon chopped fresh parsley (optional)

1. Preheat oven to 325°F. Heat oil in large skillet over medium-high heat. Add bell peppers, onion, celery and garlic; cook and stir 5 minutes or until vegetables are tender.

2. Add rice; cook and stir over medium heat 5 minutes. Add tomatoes, hot pepper sauce, oregano, salt, thyme and black pepper to skillet; stir until well blended.

3. Pour reserved tomato liquid into measuring cup; add enough water to measure 1¾ cups. Add to skillet; cook and stir 2 minutes. Stir in shrimp. Transfer to 2½-quart casserole.

4. Cover and bake 55 minutes or until rice is tender and liquid is absorbed. Garnish with parsley.

Makes 4 to 6 servings

PERFECT POT ROAST

1 tablespoon vegetable oil

1 boneless beef chuck shoulder roast (3 to 4 pounds)

6 medium potatoes, halved

6 carrots, cut into chunks

2 onions, quartered

2 stalks celery, sliced

1 can (about 14 ounces) diced tomatoes

1 teaspoon salt

1 teaspoon dried oregano

½ teaspoon black pepper

Water

1½ to 2 tablespoons all-purpose flour

Slow Cooker Directions

1. Heat oil in large skillet over medium-low heat. Add beef; cook until browned on all sides. Transfer to slow cooker.

2. Add potatoes, carrots, onions, celery, tomatoes, salt, oregano and pepper to slow cooker. Add enough water to cover bottom of slow cooker by about ½ inch.

3. Cover; cook on LOW 8 to 10 hours. Remove beef to platter; cover and let stand 15 minutes.

4. Transfer juices in slow cooker to small saucepan; whisk in flour until smooth. Cook and stir over medium heat until thickened. Slice beef; serve with gravy and vegetables.

Makes 6 to 8 servings

SOUTHERN COUNTRY CHICKEN AND BISCUITS

2 large boneless skinless chicken breasts (about 10 ounces each)

12 ounces new potatoes, diced

½ cup frozen green peas

1 jar (4 ounces) diced pimientos, drained

¼ teaspoon salt

¼ teaspoon dried thyme

⅛ teaspoon black pepper

1 can (10¾ ounces) condensed cream of chicken soup, undiluted

1 package (12 to 16 ounces) refrigerated biscuits

1. Place chicken in Dutch oven. Top with potatoes, peas and pimientos; sprinkle with salt, thyme and pepper. Spoon soup over top of mixture; bring to a boil over medium-high heat.

2. Reduce heat to low; cover and simmer 25 minutes or until chicken is no longer pink in center, turning occasionally. Remove chicken to plate; let stand until cool enough to handle.

3. Meanwhile, bake biscuits according to package directions.

4. Shred chicken with two forks. Place hot split biscuits in shallow bowl; top with chicken, vegetables and sauce.

Makes 4 servings

ZESTY SKILLET PORK CHOPS

1 teaspoon chili powder

¾ teaspoon salt, divided

4 boneless pork chops
   (about 6 ounces each)

2 cups diced tomatoes

1 cup chopped green, red
   or yellow bell pepper

¾ cup thinly sliced celery

½ cup chopped onion

1 teaspoon dried thyme

1 tablespoon hot pepper sauce

1 tablespoon vegetable oil

2 tablespoons finely chopped
   fresh parsley

1. Rub chili powder and ½ teaspoon salt evenly over one side of pork chops.

2. Combine tomatoes, bell pepper, celery, onion, thyme and hot pepper sauce in medium bowl; mix well.

3. Heat oil in large skillet over medium-high heat. Add pork, seasoned side down; cook 1 minute. Turn pork; top with tomato mixture and bring to a boil. Reduce heat to low; cover and simmer 25 minutes or until pork is tender and tomato mixture has thickened.

4. Remove pork to serving plates. Bring tomato mixture to a boil over high heat; cook 2 minutes or until most liquid has evaporated. Remove from heat; stir in parsley and remaining ¼ teaspoon salt. Spoon sauce over pork.

Makes 4 servings

SHORTCUT HOPPIN' JOHN

1 package (1 pound) andouille or smoked sausage, sliced

2½ cups chicken broth, divided

2 cans (about 15 ounces each) black-eyed peas, rinsed and drained

1 package (about 8 ounces) dirty rice mix

½ cup salsa

½ to ¾ cup lump crabmeat (optional)

Slow Cooker Directions

1. Cook sausage in large skillet over medium heat 5 minutes or until browned, stirring frequently. Transfer to slow cooker with slotted spoon; drain any drippings from skillet.

2. Return skillet to heat. Pour in ½ cup broth; cook 1 minute, scraping up browned bits from bottom of skillet. Pour over sausage. Stir black-eyed peas, rice mix, remaining broth and salsa into slow cooker with sausage.

3. Cover; cook on LOW 3 to 4 hours or until rice is tender. Add crabmeat, if desired; stir until well blended. Cover; cook on LOW about 5 minutes or until heated through.

Makes 6 servings

MEATLOAF

1 tablespoon vegetable oil	1 pound ground beef
2 green onions, minced	1 pound ground pork
¼ cup minced green bell pepper	1 cup plain dry bread crumbs
¼ cup grated carrot	2 teaspoons salt
3 cloves garlic, minced	½ teaspoon onion powder
¾ cup milk	½ teaspoon black pepper
2 eggs, beaten	½ cup ketchup, divided

1. Preheat oven to 350°F.

2. Heat oil in large skillet over medium-high heat. Add green onions, bell pepper, carrot and garlic; cook and stir 5 minutes or until vegetables are softened.

3. Whisk milk and eggs in medium bowl until well blended. Gently mix beef, pork, bread crumbs, salt, onion powder and black pepper in large bowl with hands. Add milk mixture, sautéed vegetables and ¼ cup ketchup; mix gently. Press into 9×5-inch loaf pan; place pan on rimmed baking sheet.

4. Bake 30 minutes. Spread remaining ¼ cup ketchup over meatloaf; bake 1 hour or until cooked through (160°F). Cool in pan 10 minutes; cut into slices.

Makes 6 to 8 servings

OVEN BARBECUE CHICKEN

1 cup barbecue sauce	$\frac{1}{2}$ teaspoon dry mustard
$\frac{1}{4}$ cup honey	1 cut-up whole chicken
2 tablespoons soy sauce	(about $3\frac{1}{2}$ pounds)
2 teaspoons grated fresh ginger	

1. Preheat oven to 350°F. Spray 13×9-inch baking dish with nonstick cooking spray.

2. Combine barbecue sauce, honey, soy sauce, ginger and mustard in small bowl; mix well. Place chicken in prepared baking dish; brush with sauce mixture.

3. Bake 45 minutes or until cooked through (165°F), brushing occasionally with sauce.

Makes 4 to 6 servings

CAJUN SAUSAGE AND RICE

8 ounces kielbasa sausage, cut into ¼-inch slices

1 can (about 14 ounces) diced tomatoes

1 medium onion, diced

1 medium green bell pepper, diced

2 stalks celery, thinly sliced

1 tablespoon chicken bouillon granules

1 tablespoon steak sauce

3 bay leaves *or* 1 teaspoon dried thyme

1 teaspoon sugar

¼ to ½ teaspoon hot pepper sauce

1 cup uncooked instant rice

½ cup water

½ cup chopped fresh parsley (optional)

Slow Cooker Directions

1. Combine sausage, tomatoes, onion, bell pepper, celery, bouillon, steak sauce, bay leaves, sugar and hot pepper sauce in slow cooker; mix well.

2. Cover; cook on LOW 8 hours or on HIGH 4 hours.

3. Remove and discard bay leaves. Stir in rice and water. Cover; cook on HIGH 25 minutes or until rice is tender. Stir in parsley, if desired.

Makes 4 servings

STEWED OKRA AND SHRIMP

4 ounces okra

1 tablespoon canola or vegetable oil

½ cup finely chopped onion

1 can (about 14 ounces) stewed tomatoes, undrained, chopped

1 teaspoon dried thyme

¾ teaspoon salt

¾ cup fresh corn or thawed frozen corn

½ teaspoon hot pepper sauce

4 ounces cooked baby shrimp

1. Remove and discard tip and stem ends from okra. Cut okra into ½-inch slices.

2. Heat oil in large nonstick skillet over medium heat. Add onion; cook and stir 2 minutes or until softened. Add okra; cook and stir 3 minutes. Add tomatoes with juice, thyme and salt; bring to a boil over high heat. Reduce heat to low; cover and simmer 10 minutes.

3. Add corn and hot pepper sauce; cover and simmer 10 minutes. Add shrimp; cook and stir until heated through.

Makes 4 servings

CHILI SPAGHETTI CASSEROLE

8 ounces uncooked spaghetti

1 pound ground beef

1 medium onion, chopped

¼ teaspoon salt

⅛ teaspoon black pepper

1 can (about 15 ounces) vegetarian chili with beans

1 can (about 14 ounces) Italian-style stewed tomatoes, undrained

1½ cups (6 ounces) shredded sharp Cheddar cheese, divided

½ cup sour cream

1½ teaspoons chili powder

¼ teaspoon garlic powder

1. Preheat oven to 350°F. Spray 13×9-inch baking dish with nonstick cooking spray.

2. Cook spaghetti according to package directions; drain and place in prepared baking dish.

3. Meanwhile, combine beef and onion in large skillet; season with salt and pepper. Brown beef 6 to 8 minutes over medium-high heat, stirring to break up meat. Drain fat. Stir in chili, tomatoes with juice, 1 cup cheese, sour cream, chili powder and garlic powder; mix well.

4. Add chili mixture to spaghetti; stir until well coated. Sprinkle with remaining ½ cup cheese. Cover tightly with foil.

5. Bake 30 minutes or until hot and bubbly. Let stand 5 minutes before serving.

Makes 8 servings

BIG EASY CHICKEN AND RICE

2¼ pounds chicken thighs

½ teaspoon salt

½ teaspoon paprika

½ teaspoon dried thyme

¼ teaspoon black pepper

2 tablespoons vegetable oil

½ cup chopped onion

½ cup chopped celery

½ cup chopped green bell pepper

2 cloves garlic, minced

1 cup uncooked long grain rice

1 can (about 14 ounces) diced tomatoes

1 cup water

Hot pepper sauce

1. Sprinkle chicken with salt, paprika, thyme and black pepper. Heat oil in large skillet or Dutch oven over medium heat. Add chicken; cook 5 to 6 minutes per side or until lightly browned. Remove to plate.

2. Add onion, celery, bell pepper and garlic to skillet; cook and stir 2 minutes. Add rice; cook and stir 2 minutes. Stir in tomatoes and water; season with hot pepper sauce. Bring to a boil.

3. Arrange chicken over rice mixture. Reduce heat to low; cover and cook 20 minutes or until chicken is cooked through (165°F) and liquid is absorbed.

Makes 4 servings

Sunday Suppers

CAJUN BLACKENED TUNA

2 tablespoons butter, melted

4 fresh tuna steaks (6 ounces each, about 1 inch thick)

1½ teaspoons garlic salt

1 teaspoon paprika

1 teaspoon dried thyme or oregano

½ teaspoon ground cumin

¼ teaspoon ground red pepper

⅛ teaspoon white pepper

⅛ teaspoon black pepper

4 lemon wedges

1. Prepare grill for direct cooking over medium-high heat or heat grill pan or cast iron skillet over medium-high heat.

2. Brush butter over both sides of tuna. Combine garlic salt, paprika, thyme, cumin, red pepper, white pepper and black pepper in small bowl; mix well. Sprinkle over both sides of tuna.

3. Grill tuna (or cook in preheated grill pan or skillet) 2 to 3 minutes per side for medium rare. Serve with lemon wedges.

Makes 4 servings

BUTTERMILK FRIED CHICKEN

2 cups buttermilk

1 tablespoon hot pepper sauce

3 pounds bone-in chicken pieces

2 cups all-purpose flour

2 teaspoons salt

2 teaspoons poultry seasoning

1 teaspoon garlic salt

1 teaspoon paprika

1 teaspoon ground red pepper

1 teaspoon black pepper

1 cup vegetable oil

1. Combine buttermilk and hot pepper sauce in large resealable food storage bag. Add chicken; seal bag and turn to coat. Refrigerate 2 hours or up to 24 hours.

2. Combine flour, salt, poultry seasoning, garlic salt, paprika, red pepper and black pepper in another large resealable food storage bag or shallow baking dish; mix well. Working in batches, remove chicken from buttermilk; shake off excess. Add to flour mixture; shake to coat.

3. Heat oil to 350°F in large skillet over medium heat; adjust heat to maintain temperature. Working in batches, cook chicken 30 minutes or until cooked through (165°F), turning occasionally to brown all sides. Drain on paper towel-lined plate.

Makes 4 servings

TIP: Carefully monitor the temperature of the oil during cooking; it should not drop below 325°F or go higher than 350°F. The chicken can also be cooked in a deep fryer according to the manufacturer's directions.

SKILLET TILAPIA WITH RICE AND BEANS

2 tablespoons all-purpose flour

½ teaspoon salt, divided

⅛ teaspoon black pepper

4 tilapia fillets (4 to 6 ounces each), patted dry

2 tablespoons butter, divided

1 can (about 15 ounces) black beans, rinsed and drained

1 can (about 14 ounces) diced tomatoes with chiles

1 package (about 8 ounces) ready-to-serve Spanish rice

¼ teaspoon dried oregano

1 green onion, finely chopped

1. Combine flour, ¼ teaspoon salt and pepper in large resealable food storage bag; mix well. Add tilapia; seal bag and shake to coat.

2. Melt 1 tablespoon butter in large skillet over medium-high heat. Add tilapia; cook 2 minutes per side or until golden brown and fish begins to flake when tested with fork. Remove to plate; tent with foil to keep warm.

3. Melt remaining 1 tablespoon butter in same skillet over medium-high heat. Stir in beans, tomatoes, rice, oregano and remaining ¼ teaspoon salt. Reduce heat to low; cook 5 minutes, stirring frequently.

4. Arrange tilapia over rice mixture. Sprinkle with green onion.

Makes 4 servings

OLD-FASHIONED CHICKEN AND DUMPLINGS

3 tablespoons butter

3 to 3½ pounds bone-in chicken pieces

3 cans (about 14 ounces each) chicken broth

3½ cups water

1 teaspoon salt

¼ teaspoon white pepper

2 large carrots, cut into 1-inch slices

2 stalks celery, cut into 1-inch slices

8 to 10 pearl onions, peeled

4 ounces small mushrooms, cut into halves

Parsley Dumplings (recipe follows)

½ cup frozen green peas, thawed and drained

1. Melt butter in Dutch oven over medium-high heat. Add chicken; cook until golden brown on all sides.

2. Add broth, water, salt and pepper; bring to a boil over high heat. Reduce heat to low; cover and simmer 15 minutes. Add carrots, celery, onions and mushrooms; cover and simmer 40 minutes or until chicken and vegetables are tender.

3. Prepare Parsley Dumplings. When chicken is tender, skim fat from broth. Stir in peas. Drop dumpling mixture into broth, making 12 dumplings. Cover and simmer 15 to 20 minutes or until dumplings are firm to the touch and toothpick inserted into centers comes out clean.

Makes 6 servings

PARSLEY DUMPLINGS: Sift 2 cups all-purpose flour, 4 teaspoons baking powder and 1 teaspoon salt into medium bowl. Cut in 5 tablespoons cold butter with pastry blender or two knives until mixture resembles coarse meal. Make well in center; pour in 1 cup milk. Add 2 tablespoons chopped fresh parsley; stir with fork until mixture forms a ball.

SPICED HONEY GLAZED HAM

1 smoked bone-in spiral-cut ham (about 8 pounds)

½ cup clover honey or other mild honey

2 tablespoons spicy brown mustard

2 tablespoons cider vinegar

1 teaspoon finely grated orange peel

¼ teaspoon black pepper

⅛ teaspoon ground cloves

1. Position rack in lower third of oven. Preheat oven to 325°F.

2. Line large rimmed baking pan with heavy-duty foil; place wire rack over foil. Place ham on rack; cover loosely with foil. Pour 2 cups water into pan. Bake 1½ hours.

3. Meanwhile, prepare glaze. Combine honey, mustard, vinegar, orange peel, pepper and cloves in small saucepan; bring to a boil over medium-high heat. Remove from heat; set aside to cool.

4. Remove ham from oven. *Increase oven temperature to 400°F.* Brush ham with glaze; bake, uncovered, 40 minutes or until shiny golden brown crust has formed, brushing with glaze every 10 minutes.

5. Transfer ham to cutting board. Let stand 10 minutes before slicing.

Makes 12 to 14 servings

SPICY SHRIMP GUMBO

½ cup vegetable oil

½ cup all-purpose flour

1 large onion, chopped

½ cup chopped fresh parsley

½ cup chopped celery

½ cup sliced green onions

6 cloves garlic, minced

4 cups chicken broth or water*

1 package (10 ounces) frozen sliced okra, thawed (optional)

1 teaspoon salt

½ teaspoon ground red pepper

2 pounds medium raw shrimp, peeled and deveined

3 cups hot cooked rice

Fresh parsley sprigs (optional)

Traditional gumbo is thick like stew. For thinner gumbo, add 1 to 2 cups additional broth.

1. For roux, blend oil and flour in large saucepan or Dutch oven until smooth. Cook over medium heat 10 to 15 minutes or until roux is dark brown but not burned, stirring frequently.

2. Add chopped onion, chopped parsley, celery, green onions and garlic to roux; cook 5 to 10 minutes or until vegetables are tender, stirring frequently. Add broth, okra, if desired, salt and red pepper; cover and cook 15 minutes.

3. Add shrimp; cook 3 to 5 minutes or until shrimp turn pink and opaque.

4. Place about ⅓ cup rice into eight wide-rimmed bowls; top with gumbo. Garnish with parsley sprigs.

Makes 8 servings

SMOKY BABY BACK RIBS

1¼ cups water

1 cup white vinegar

⅔ cup packed dark brown sugar

½ cup tomato paste

1 tablespoon yellow mustard

1½ teaspoons salt

1 teaspoon liquid smoke

1 teaspoon onion powder

½ teaspoon garlic powder

½ teaspoon paprika

2 racks pork baby back ribs
  (3½ to 4 pounds total)

1. Combine water, vinegar, brown sugar, tomato paste, mustard, salt, liquid smoke, onion powder, garlic powder and paprika in medium saucepan; bring to a boil over medium heat. Reduce heat to medium-low; cook 40 minutes or until sauce thickens, stirring occasionally.

2. Preheat oven to 300°F. Place each rack of ribs on large sheet of heavy-duty foil. Brush some of sauce over ribs, covering completely. Fold down edges of foil tightly to seal and create packet; arrange packets on baking sheet, seam sides up.

3. Bake 2 hours. Preheat broiler. Carefully open packets and drain off excess liquid.

4. Brush ribs with sauce; broil 5 minutes per side or until ribs begin to char, brushing with sauce once or twice. Serve with remaining sauce.

Makes 4 servings

SOUTHERN-STYLE CHICKEN AND GREENS

1 teaspoon salt

1 teaspoon paprika

½ teaspoon black pepper

3½ pounds bone-in chicken pieces

4 slices thick-cut smoked bacon, cut into ¼-inch pieces

1 cup uncooked rice

1 can (about 14 ounces) stewed tomatoes, undrained

1¼ cups chicken broth

2 cups packed coarsely chopped collard greens, mustard greens or kale (3 to 4 ounces)

1. Preheat oven to 350°F. Combine salt, paprika and pepper in small bowl; sprinkle over chicken.

2. Cook bacon in Dutch oven over medium heat until crisp. Drain on paper towel-lined plate. Working in batches, add chicken to drippings in Dutch oven; cook 5 minutes per side or until browned. (Cook chicken in single layer; do not crowd.) Remove to plate. Drain all but 1 tablespoon drippings from Dutch oven.

3. Add rice to drippings in Dutch oven; cook and stir 1 minute. Add tomatoes with juice, broth, collard greens and half of bacon; bring to a boil over high heat. Remove from heat; arrange chicken over rice mixture.

4. Cover and bake about 40 minutes or until chicken is cooked through (165°F) and most liquid is absorbed. Let stand 5 minutes before serving. Sprinkle with remaining bacon.

Makes 4 to 6 servings

SERVING SUGGESTION: Serve with corn bread or corn muffins.

PAN-FRIED CATFISH WITH HUSH PUPPIES

Hush Puppy Batter
(page 127)

4 catfish fillets
(about 6 ounces each)

½ cup yellow cornmeal

3 tablespoons all-purpose
flour

1½ teaspoons salt

¼ teaspoon ground red pepper

Vegetable oil

1. Prepare Hush Puppy Batter; set aside.

2. Rinse catfish; pat dry with paper towels. Combine cornmeal, flour, salt and red pepper in shallow dish; mix well. Dip fish in cornmeal mixture; turn to coat.

3. Heat 1 inch oil in large skillet over medium heat to 375°F; adjust heat to maintain temperature.

4. Cook catfish in batches 4 to 5 minutes or until golden brown and fish begins to flake when tested with fork. Drain on paper towel-lined plate; tent with foil to keep warm. *Allow temperature of oil to return to 375°F between batches.*

5. Drop hush puppy batter by tablespoonfuls into hot oil (375°F). Cook, in batches, 2 minutes or until golden brown. Drain on paper towel-lined plate. Serve warm with catfish.

Makes 4 servings

HUSH PUPPY BATTER

1½ cups yellow cornmeal

½ cup all-purpose flour

2 teaspoons baking powder

½ teaspoon salt

1 cup milk

1 small onion, minced

1 egg, lightly beaten

Combine cornmeal, flour, baking powder and salt in medium bowl; mix well. Add milk, onion and egg; stir until well blended. Let batter stand 5 to 10 minutes.

Makes about 24 hush puppies

FRENCH DIP SANDWICHES

3 pounds boneless beef
    chuck roast

½ teaspoon salt

½ teaspoon black pepper

1 tablespoon olive oil

2 large onions, cut into halves,
    then cut into ¼-inch slices

2¼ cups reduced-sodium beef
    broth, divided

3 tablespoons Worcestershire
    sauce

6 hoagie rolls, split

12 slices provolone cheese

1. Season beef with salt and pepper. Heat oil in Dutch oven or large saucepan over medium-high heat. Add beef; cook about 6 minutes per side or until browned. Remove to plate.

2. Add onions and ¼ cup broth to Dutch oven; cook 8 minutes or until golden brown, stirring occasionally and scraping up browned bits from bottom of pan. Remove half of onions to small bowl; set aside. Stir in remaining 2 cups broth and Worcestershire sauce; mix well. Return beef to Dutch oven. Reduce heat to low; cover and simmer 3 to 3½ hours or until beef is fork-tender.

3. Remove beef to large bowl; let stand until cool enough to handle. Shred into bite-size pieces. Add ⅔ cup cooking liquid; toss to coat. Pour remaining cooking liquid into small bowl for serving. Preheat broiler or toaster oven. Line baking sheet with foil.

4. Place rolls cut side up on prepared baking sheet; broil until lightly browned. Top bottom halves of rolls with cheese, beef and reserved onions. Serve with warm au jus for dipping.

Makes 6 servings

CHICKEN AND SAUSAGE JAMBALAYA

1½ tablespoons vegetable oil, divided

12 ounces boneless skinless chicken breasts, cut into 1-inch pieces

12 to 14 ounces andouille sausage or other smoked sausage, cut into ¼-inch slices

1 onion, chopped

½ red bell pepper, diced

½ green bell pepper, diced

1½ tablespoons Cajun seasoning

3 cloves garlic, minced

¾ teaspoon dried thyme

1 can (about 14 ounces) diced tomatoes

2 bay leaves

½ teaspoon salt

2¾ cups chicken broth

1½ cups uncooked rice

Sliced green onions or chopped fresh parsley (optional)

1. Heat 1 tablespoon oil in large saucepan or Dutch oven over medium-high heat. Add chicken; cook about 5 minutes or until browned, stirring occasionally. Remove to plate.

2. Add remaining ½ tablespoon oil and sausage to saucepan; cook 5 minutes or until browned, stirring occasionally. Remove to plate with chicken. Add onion and bell peppers to saucepan; cook 3 minutes or until vegetables are softened, scraping up browned bits from bottom of pan. Add Cajun seasoning, garlic and thyme; cook and stir 1 minute. Add tomatoes, bay leaves and salt; mix well. Stir in broth, rice, chicken and sausage; bring to a boil.

3. Reduce heat to low; cover and simmer 30 minutes or until rice is tender and liquid is absorbed. Stir rice; remove and discard bay leaves. Top with green onions, if desired.

Makes 6 to 8 servings

TRI-TIP ROAST WITH SPICY POTATOES

4 teaspoons chili powder	3 tablespoons lime juice, divided
2 teaspoons dried oregano	1 tablespoon olive oil
1 teaspoon salt	1 boneless beef loin tri-tip roast (about 1¾ pounds)
3 pounds unpeeled red potatoes (about 9 medium)	

1. Preheat oven to 455°F. Spray 13×9-inch baking dish with nonstick cooking spray. Combine chili powder, oregano and salt in small bowl; mix well.

2. Cut potatoes into wedges; place in large bowl. Add 2 tablespoons lime juice, oil and 1 tablespoon spice mixture; toss to coat. Spread potatoes in single layer in prepared baking dish.

3. Brush beef with remaining 1 tablespoon lime juice; rub with remaining spice mixture. Place beef on rack in roasting pan.

4. Roast 10 minutes. Place potatoes beside or below beef in oven; roast 40 to 50 minutes or until temperature in center of roast reaches 150°F. Remove beef and potatoes from oven; tent with foil to keep warm. Let beef stand 10 minutes before carving. (Temperature will rise about 10° during standing.)

5. Thinly slice beef across the grain. Serve with potatoes.

Makes 6 servings

CORNISH HENS WITH ANDOUILLE STUFFING

4 Cornish game hens (about 1¼ pounds each), thawed if frozen

6 tablespoons (¾ stick) butter, divided

2 links (8 ounces) fully cooked andouille or chicken andouille sausage, chopped

1 cup chopped onion

½ cup thinly sliced celery

1¼ to 1½ cups water

1 package (8 ounces) herb stuffing mix

1 teaspoon dried thyme

1 teaspoon paprika or smoked paprika

1 teaspoon garlic salt

¼ teaspoon black pepper

1 cup cranberry chutney or whole-berry cranberry sauce

1. Preheat oven to 375°F. Spray 3-quart baking dish with nonstick cooking spray. Pat Cornish hens dry with paper towels.

2. Melt 2 tablespoons butter in large saucepan over medium heat. Add sausage, onion and celery; cook 8 to 10 minutes or until vegetables are tender and sausage is browned, stirring occasionally. Add water (use 1½ cups water for a moister stuffing); bring to a boil. Remove from heat; add stuffing mix and stir to blend.

3. Spoon ½ cup stuffing into each hen cavity. Place hens on rack in shallow roasting pan. Tie legs together, if desired. Place remaining stuffing in prepared baking dish.

4. Melt remaining 4 tablespoons butter. Add thyme, paprika, garlic salt and pepper; mix well. Spoon half of butter mixture over hens. Roast hens 30 minutes. Bake remaining stuffing with hens 25 minutes. Brush remaining butter mixture over hens; roast 20 to 25 minutes or until hens are cooked through (165°F). Serve hens and stuffing with cranberry chutney.

Makes 4 servings

Side Dishes

CLASSIC MACARONI AND CHEESE

2 cups uncooked elbow macaroni

¼ cup (½ stick) butter

¼ cup all-purpose flour

2½ cups whole milk

1 teaspoon salt

⅛ teaspoon black pepper

4 cups (16 ounces) shredded Colby-Jack cheese

1. Cook pasta in medium saucepan of salted boiling water according to package directions until al dente. Drain and set aside.

2. Melt butter in large saucepan over medium heat. Add flour; whisk until well blended and bubbly. Gradually add milk, salt and pepper, whisking until blended. Cook and stir until milk begins to bubble. Add cheese, 1 cup at a time; cook and stir until cheese is melted and sauce is smooth.

3. Add cooked pasta to saucepan; stir gently until blended. Cook until heated through.

Makes 8 servings (about 8 cups)

COLLARD GREENS WITH BACON

4 slices thick-cut bacon,
    cut into ½-inch pieces

1 pound collard greens,
    stems trimmed,
    roughly chopped
    (1- to 2-inch pieces)

1 cup chicken broth or water

1 tablespoon cider vinegar

1 tablespoon packed brown
    sugar

¼ teaspoon salt

¼ teaspoon black pepper

¼ teaspoon red pepper flakes

1. Cook bacon in large saucepan or Dutch oven over medium-high heat until crisp. Add greens; cook and stir until wilted.

2. Add broth, vinegar, brown sugar, salt, black pepper and red pepper flakes; bring to a simmer. Reduce heat to medium-low; cover and cook 45 to 55 minutes or until greens are tender.

Makes 4 to 6 servings

SCALLOPED POTATOES WITH HAM

2 tablespoons butter

1 tablespoon all-purpose flour

¾ teaspoon salt

¼ teaspoon black pepper

1¼ cups whipping cream

1¼ cups whole milk

2 cups (8 ounces) shredded Swiss cheese, divided

1½ pounds russet potatoes

1 medium onion, cut into thin rings and separated

8 ounces cubed or sliced baked ham

1. Melt butter in medium saucepan over medium heat. Whisk in flour, salt and pepper; cook 1 minute. Gradually whisk in cream and milk; bring to a boil. Remove from heat; stir in 1½ cups cheese in two or three batches. Set aside.

2. Preheat oven to 350°F. Spray 12×8-inch baking dish with nonstick cooking spray.

3. Peel potatoes and cut into ⅛-inch-thick slices. Layer one third of potato slices, half of onion slices and one third of sauce in prepared baking dish. Top with one third of potato slices, remaining onion, ham, one third of sauce and remaining potato slices and sauce. Cover baking dish with foil.

4. Bake 50 to 55 minutes or until potatoes are almost tender. Sprinkle with remaining ½ cup cheese. Bake 10 to 15 minutes or until cheese is golden brown. Let stand 10 minutes before serving.

Makes about 6 servings

MEATY BAKED BEANS

8 ounces ground beef

1 small onion, chopped

8 slices bacon, chopped

1 can (about 15 ounces) pinto beans, rinsed and drained

1 can (about 15 ounces) butter beans, rinsed and drained, ¼ cup liquid reserved

1 can (about 15 ounces) kidney beans, rinsed and drained

¼ cup ketchup

2 tablespoons molasses

½ teaspoon dry mustard

½ cup granulated sugar

¼ cup packed brown sugar

Slow Cooker Directions

1. Brown ground beef, onion and bacon in medium saucepan over high heat. Stir in beans and reserved liquid.

2. Combine ketchup, molasses and dry mustard in medium bowl; mix well. Add granulated sugar and brown sugar; stir until well blended. Add to beef mixture; mix well. Transfer to slow cooker.

3. Cover; cook on LOW 2 to 3 hours or until heated through.

Makes 6 to 8 servings

HONEY BUTTER PULL-APART BREAD

3 cups all-purpose flour

1 package (¼ ounce) instant
    yeast

1 teaspoon salt

1 cup warm water (120°F)

2 tablespoons butter, melted

¼ cup (½ stick) butter, softened

¼ cup honey

1. Combine flour, yeast and salt in large bowl of stand mixer. Stir in warm water and
   2 tablespoons melted butter with spoon or spatula to form rough dough. Mix with
   dough hook at low speed 5 to 7 minutes or until dough is smooth and elastic.

2. Shape dough into a ball. Place in greased bowl; turn to grease top. Cover and let rise
   in warm place 45 minutes to 1 hour or until doubled in size.

3. Spray 8×4-inch loaf pan with nonstick cooking spray. Combine ¼ cup softened butter
   and honey in small bowl; mix well.

4. Turn out dough onto lightly floured surface. Roll out dough into 18×10-inch rectangle;
   cut in half crosswise to make two 9×10-inch rectangles. Spread one third of honey
   butter over one half of dough; top with remaining half of dough. Cut dough in half
   crosswise to make two 9×5-inch rectangles. Spread one third of honey butter over
   one half of dough; top with remaining half of dough. Cut dough in half lengthwise,
   then cut crosswise into 1-inch strips. Place rows of strips vertically in prepared pan.
   Cover and let rise in warm place 1 hour or until dough is puffy. Preheat oven to 350°F.
   Brush or dollop remaining one third of honey butter over dough strips.

5. Bake 30 minutes or until bread is firm and golden brown. Remove to wire rack to cool
   slightly. Serve warm.

Makes 8 servings

FRUITED CORN PUDDING

5 cups thawed frozen corn, divided

5 eggs

½ cup milk

1½ cups whipping cream

⅓ cup butter, melted and cooled

1 teaspoon vanilla

½ teaspoon salt

¼ teaspoon ground nutmeg

3 tablespoons finely chopped dried apricots

3 tablespoons dried cranberries or raisins

3 tablespoons finely chopped dates

2 tablespoons finely chopped dried pears or other dried fruit

1. Preheat oven to 350°F. Spray 13×9-inch baking dish with nonstick cooking spray.

2. Combine 3½ cups corn, eggs and milk in food processor; process until almost smooth.

3. Transfer corn mixture to large bowl. Add cream, butter, vanilla, salt and nutmeg; stir until well blended. Add remaining 1½ cups corn, apricots, cranberries, dates and pears; mix well. Pour into prepared baking dish.

4. Bake 50 to 60 minutes or until center is set and top begins to brown. Let stand 10 to 15 minutes before serving.

Makes 8 servings

SPICY BLACK-EYED PEAS WITH HAM HOCKS

6 cups water

2 ham hocks (about 1 pound)

2 pounds frozen black-eyed peas

½ cup chopped onion

½ medium jalapeño pepper, stemmed and cut into rings*

2 teaspoons salt

Sliced green onions (optional)

If discarding seeds, use 1 whole jalapeño pepper instead.

1. Bring water to a boil in Dutch oven over high heat. Add ham hocks, black-eyed peas, onion, jalapeño pepper and salt; return to a boil. Reduce heat to low; simmer, uncovered, 30 minutes or until peas are very tender and mixture begins to thicken slightly.

2. Remove from heat and remove ham hocks. Let peas stand 20 minutes before serving to thicken slightly. Garnish with green onions.

Makes 6 servings

SOUR CREAM GARLIC MASHED POTATOES

2 pounds red potatoes, peeled*
   and cut into 1-inch pieces

6 cloves garlic, peeled

¼ cup (½ stick) butter

1 cup sour cream

1 teaspoon salt

½ teaspoon white pepper

For more texture, leave the potatoes unpeeled.

1. Place potatoes and garlic in large saucepan; cover with water and bring to a boil over high heat. Reduce heat to low; cook 20 minutes or until potatoes are tender. Drain.

2. Return potatoes to saucepan. Add butter; mash with potato masher until smooth and butter is melted. Stir in sour cream, salt and pepper until well blended.

Makes 8 servings

CHORIZO AND CORN DRESSING

8 ounces chorizo sausage, casings removed

1 can (about 14 ounces) reduced-sodium chicken broth

1 can (10¾ ounces) condensed cream of chicken soup, undiluted

1 package (6 ounces) corn bread stuffing mix

1 cup chopped onion

1 cup diced red bell pepper

1 cup chopped celery

1 cup frozen corn

3 eggs, lightly beaten

Slow Cooker Directions

1. Spray inside of slow cooker with nonstick cooking spray.

2. Cook chorizo in large skillet over medium-high heat until browned, stirring to break up meat. Transfer to slow cooker.

3. Whisk broth and soup into drippings in skillet over low heat. Add stuffing mix, onion, bell pepper, celery, corn and eggs; stir until well blended. Stir into slow cooker.

4. Cover; cook on LOW 7 hours or on HIGH 3½ hours.

Makes 4 to 6 servings

NO-FUSS DIRTY RICE

8 ounces bulk Italian sausage

2 cups water

1 cup uncooked long grain rice

1 large onion, finely chopped

1 large green bell pepper, finely chopped

$\frac{1}{2}$ cup finely chopped celery

$1\frac{1}{2}$ teaspoons salt

$\frac{1}{2}$ teaspoon ground red pepper

$\frac{1}{2}$ cup chopped fresh parsley

Slow Cooker Directions

1. Brown sausage in large skillet over medium-high heat 6 to 8 minutes, stirring to break up meat. Drain fat.

2. Transfer sausage to slow cooker. Stir in water, rice, onion, bell pepper, celery, salt and red pepper; mix well.

3. Cover; cook on LOW 2 hours. Stir in parsley.

Makes 4 servings

COCONUT-PECAN SWEET POTATO CASSEROLE

2 cans (15 ounces each) sweet potatoes in heavy syrup, drained

$\frac{1}{2}$ cup (1 stick) butter, softened

$\frac{1}{4}$ cup packed brown sugar

1 egg

$\frac{1}{2}$ teaspoon vanilla

$\frac{1}{8}$ teaspoon salt

$\frac{1}{2}$ cup chopped pecans

$\frac{1}{4}$ cup flaked coconut

2 tablespoons golden raisins

1. Preheat oven to 325°F. Spray 8-inch square baking dish with nonstick cooking spray.

2. Combine sweet potatoes, butter, brown sugar, egg, vanilla and salt in food processor or blender; process until smooth. Spoon into prepared baking dish. Sprinkle with pecans, coconut and raisins.

3. Bake 22 to 25 minutes or until heated through and coconut is lightly browned.

Makes 4 servings

GARLICKY MUSTARD GREENS

2 pounds mustard greens

1 tablespoon olive oil

1 cup chopped onion

2 cloves garlic, minced

¾ cup chopped red bell pepper

½ cup chicken or vegetable broth

1 tablespoon cider vinegar

1 teaspoon sugar

1. Remove stems and any wilted leaves from greens. Stack several leaves; roll up and cut crosswise into 1-inch slices. Repeat with remaining greens.

2. Heat oil in large saucepan over medium heat. Add onion and garlic; cook and stir 5 minutes or until onion is tender. Stir in greens, bell pepper and broth. Reduce heat to low; cover and cook 25 minutes or until greens are tender, stirring occasionally.

3. Combine vinegar and sugar in small bowl; stir until sugar is dissolved. Stir into cooked greens; remove from heat. Serve immediately.

Makes 4 servings

Southern-Style Sweets

CHERRY SODA POKE CAKE

1 package (about 15 ounces) white cake mix, plus ingredients to prepare mix

1 package (4-serving size) cherry gelatin

¾ cup boiling water

Ice cubes

½ cup cherry-flavored cola

1 container (8 ounces) frozen whipped topping, thawed

3 tablespoons maraschino cherry juice (optional)

½ cup maraschino cherries

1. Prepare and bake cake according to package directions for 13×9-inch pan. Cool completely in pan on wire rack.

2. Poke holes in cake at ½-inch intervals with round wooden spoon handle. Combine gelatin and boiling water in small bowl; stir until gelatin is dissolved. Add enough ice to cola to measure 1¼ cups; stir into gelatin mixture. Chill gelatin 15 minutes. Stir gelatin; pour over cake.

3. Combine whipped topping and cherry juice, if desired, in medium bowl. Spread whipped topping over cake; top with cherries. Refrigerate 2 to 3 hours or until firm.

Makes 12 to 15 servings

BANANA CREAM PIE

1 refrigerated pie crust (half
   of 14-ounce package)

²⁄₃ cup sugar

¼ cup cornstarch

¼ teaspoon salt

2½ cups milk

4 egg yolks, beaten

2 tablespoons butter, softened

2 teaspoons vanilla

2 medium bananas

1 teaspoon lemon juice

   Whipped cream and toasted
    sliced almonds (optional)

1. Let crust stand at room temperature 15 minutes. Preheat oven to 400°F.

2. Line 9-inch pie plate with crust; flute edge. Prick bottom and side all over with fork. Bake 10 minutes or until crust is golden brown. Cool completely on wire rack.

3. Combine sugar, cornstarch and salt in medium saucepan; whisk in milk until well blended. Cook over medium heat about 12 minutes or until mixture boils and thickens, stirring constantly. Boil 2 minutes, stirring constantly. Remove from heat.

4. Gradually whisk ½ hot cup milk mixture into egg yolks in small bowl. Gradually whisk mixture back into milk mixture in saucepan. Cook over medium heat about 5 minutes, whisking constantly. Remove from heat; whisk in butter and vanilla. Cool 20 minutes, stirring occasionally. Strain through fine-mesh strainer into medium bowl. Press plastic wrap onto surface of pudding; cool about 30 minutes or until lukewarm.

5. Cut bananas into ¼-inch slices; toss with lemon juice in medium bowl. Spread half of pudding in cooled crust; arrange bananas over pudding. (Reserve several slices for garnish, if desired.) Spread remaining pudding over bananas. Refrigerate 4 hours or overnight. Garnish with whipped cream, almonds and reserved banana slices.

Makes 8 servings

DOUBLE CHOCOLATE PECAN BROWNIES

1 cup plus 2 tablespoons all-purpose flour

$\frac{3}{4}$ cup unsweetened cocoa powder

$\frac{1}{2}$ teaspoon baking powder

$\frac{1}{4}$ teaspoon salt

$1\frac{1}{4}$ cups sugar

$\frac{1}{2}$ cup (1 stick) butter, softened

2 eggs

1 teaspoon vanilla

$\frac{1}{2}$ cup semisweet chocolate chips

$\frac{1}{2}$ cup chopped pecans

1. Preheat oven to 350°F. Line 8-inch square baking pan with foil, extending foil over two sides of pan. Spray foil with nonstick cooking spray.

2. Combine flour, cocoa, baking powder and salt in medium bowl; mix well. Beat sugar and butter in large bowl with electric mixer at medium speed 2 to 3 minutes or until creamy. Add eggs, one at a time, beating well after each addition. Beat in vanilla. Gradually add flour mixture at low speed, beating just until blended. Spread batter in prepared pan (batter will be very thick). Sprinkle with chocolate chips and pecans.

3. Bake about 30 minutes or until toothpick inserted into center comes out almost clean. Cool in pan 5 minutes; use foil to remove brownies to wire rack to cool completely. Cut into bars.

Makes 16 brownies

BROWN BUTTER
BLUEBERRY PEACH COBBLER

3 tablespoons butter

4 packages (16 ounces each) frozen sliced peaches, thawed and drained

1 cup fresh blueberries

1/2 cup packed brown sugar

1/4 cup all-purpose flour

1/2 teaspoon vanilla

1/4 teaspoon ground nutmeg

1 1/4 cups pancake and baking mix

1/3 cup milk

2 tablespoons butter, melted

2 tablespoons granulated sugar

1. Preheat oven to 375°F.

2. Melt 3 tablespoons butter in large skillet (not nonstick) over medium heat. Cook and stir 3 minutes or until butter has nutty aroma and turns light brown in color. Add peaches; cook and stir 2 minutes.

3. Combine peaches, blueberries, brown sugar, flour, vanilla and nutmeg in large bowl; toss gently to coat. Spoon into 2-quart oval baking dish.

4. Bake 10 minutes. Meanwhile, combine baking mix, milk, 2 tablespoons melted butter and granulated sugar in medium bowl; mix well. Drop batter in eight equal spoonfuls over warm fruit mixture.

5. Bake 30 to 35 minutes or until topping is deep golden brown and cooked on bottom. Cool 10 minutes. Serve warm.

Makes 8 servings

SWEET POTATO PECAN PIE

1 large sweet potato (about 1 pound)

3 eggs, divided

8 tablespoons granulated sugar, divided

8 tablespoons packed brown sugar, divided

2 tablespoons butter, melted, divided

½ teaspoon ground cinnamon

½ teaspoon salt, divided

1 frozen 9-inch deep-dish pie crust

½ cup dark corn syrup

1½ teaspoons lemon juice

1½ teaspoons vanilla

1 cup pecan halves

Vanilla ice cream (optional)

1. Preheat oven to 350°F. Prick sweet potato all over with fork. Bake 1 hour or until fork-tender; let stand until cool enough to handle. Peel sweet potato and place in bowl of stand mixer. *Reduce oven temperature to 300°F.*

2. Add 1 egg, 2 tablespoons granulated sugar, 2 tablespoons brown sugar, 1 tablespoon butter, cinnamon and ¼ teaspoon salt to bowl with sweet potato; beat at medium speed 5 minutes or until smooth and fluffy. Spread mixture in frozen pie crust; place in refrigerator.

3. Combine remaining 6 tablespoons granulated sugar, 6 tablespoons brown sugar, 1 tablespoon butter, ¼ teaspoon salt, corn syrup, lemon juice and vanilla in clean mixer bowl; beat at medium speed 5 minutes. Add remaining 2 eggs; beat 5 minutes. Place crust on baking sheet. Spread pecans over sweet potato filling; pour corn syrup mixture evenly over pecans.

4. Bake 1 hour or until center is set and top is deep golden brown. Cool completely on wire rack. Serve with ice cream, if desired.

Makes 8 servings

RED VELVET CAKE

Cake

- 2 cups all-purpose flour
- 2 tablespoons unsweetened cocoa powder
- 1 teaspoon salt
- 1¼ cups buttermilk
- 1 bottle (1 ounce) red food coloring
- 1 teaspoon vanilla
- 1½ cups granulated sugar
- 1 cup (2 sticks) butter, softened
- 2 eggs
- 1 tablespoon white or cider vinegar
- 1½ teaspoons baking soda

Frosting

- 2 packages (8 ounces each) cream cheese, softened
- ½ cup (1 stick) butter, softened
- 6 cups powdered sugar
- ¼ cup milk
- 2 teaspoons vanilla
- 4 ounces white chocolate, shaved with vegetable peeler

1. Preheat oven to 350°F. Spray three 9-inch cake pans with nonstick cooking spray. Line bottoms of pans with parchment paper; spray parchment with cooking spray.

2. For cake, combine flour, cocoa and salt in medium bowl. Combine buttermilk, food coloring and vanilla in small bowl; mix well.

3. Beat granulated sugar and 1 cup butter in large bowl with electric mixer at medium speed 5 minutes or until light and fluffy. Add eggs, one at a time, beating until well blended after each addition. Add flour mixture alternately with buttermilk mixture, beating at low speed after each addition. Stir vinegar into baking soda in small bowl. Add to batter; stir gently until blended. Pour batter into prepared pans.

4. Bake about 20 minutes or until toothpick inserted into centers comes out clean. Cool in pans 10 minutes. Invert onto wire racks; peel off parchment. Cool completely.

5. For frosting, beat cream cheese and ½ cup butter in large bowl with electric mixer at medium speed until creamy. Add powdered sugar, milk and 2 teaspoons vanilla; beat at low speed until blended. Beat at medium speed until smooth.

6. Place one cake layer on serving plate; spread with 1½ cups frosting. Top with second cake layer; spread with 1½ cups frosting. Top with remaining cake layer; spread remaining frosting over top and side of cake. Press white chocolate shavings onto side of cake.

Makes 8 to 10 servings

SNICKERDOODLES

¾ cup plus 2 tablespoons sugar, divided

2 teaspoons ground cinnamon, divided

1⅓ cups all-purpose flour

1 teaspoon cream of tartar

½ teaspoon baking soda

½ teaspoon salt

½ cup (1 stick) butter, softened

1 egg

1. Preheat oven to 375°F. Line cookie sheets with parchment paper. Combine 2 tablespoons sugar and 1 teaspoon cinnamon in small bowl.

2. Combine flour, remaining 1 teaspoon cinnamon, cream of tartar, baking soda and salt in medium bowl; mix well.

3. Beat remaining ¾ cup sugar and butter in large bowl with electric mixer at medium speed about 3 minutes or until creamy. Beat in egg until well blended. Gradually add flour mixture, beating at low speed until stiff dough forms. Roll dough into 1-inch balls; roll in cinnamon-sugar mixture to coat. Place on prepared cookie sheets.

4. Bake 10 minutes or until cookies are set. *Do not overbake.* Remove to wire racks to cool completely.

Makes about 3 dozen cookies

LIME CHIFFON PIE

1 cup sugar, divided

1 envelope (1 tablespoon) unflavored gelatin

⅛ teaspoon salt

1 cup cola

3 eggs, separated

¼ cup lime juice

¼ cup dark rum *or* 1 tablespoon rum extract

1 cup thawed frozen whipped topping or whipped cream

1 (9-inch) graham cracker or chocolate cookie crust

2 tablespoons grated lime peel

1. Combine ½ cup sugar, gelatin and salt in top of double boiler. Stir in cola until blended.

2. Whisk egg yolks in small bowl; stir into gelatin mixture. Cook over boiling water about 5 minutes or until gelatin is dissolved, stirring constantly. Remove pan from boiling water; stir in lime juice and rum. Refrigerate until mixture mounds when dropped from spoon.

3. Beat egg whites in large bowl with electric mixer until soft peaks form. Gradually beat in remaining ½ cup sugar; beat until stiff and glossy. Gently fold gelatin mixture into whipped topping in medium bowl, then fold into egg whites. Refrigerate 5 minutes before spreading in crust.

4. Sprinkle pie with lime peel. Refrigerate several hours or until firm.

Makes 6 servings

PECAN PRALINE BRANDY CAKE

1 package (about 15 ounces) butter pecan cake mix	1 cup chopped toasted pecans,* divided
¾ cup water	⅔ cup packed brown sugar
⅓ cup plain yogurt	⅓ cup light corn syrup
2 egg whites	¼ cup whipping cream
1 egg	2 tablespoons butter
¼ cup plus ½ teaspoon brandy, divided	½ teaspoon vanilla
2 tablespoons vegetable oil	

To toast pecans, spread on baking sheet. Bake in preheated 350°F oven 8 to 10 minutes or until lightly browned, stirring frequently.

1. Preheat oven to 350°F. Spray 10- or 12-cup bundt pan with nonstick cooking spray.

2. Beat cake mix, water, yogurt, egg whites, egg, ¼ cup brandy and oil in medium bowl with electric mixer at low speed 30 seconds. Beat at medium speed 2 minutes or until light and fluffy. Fold in ½ cup pecans. Pour batter into prepared pan.

3. Bake 50 minutes or until toothpick inserted near center comes out clean. Cool in pan 10 minutes; invert onto wire rack to cool completely.

4. Combine brown sugar, corn syrup, cream and butter in small saucepan; bring to a boil over medium heat, stirring constantly. Remove from heat; stir in remaining ½ cup pecans, ½ teaspoon brandy and vanilla. Cool to room temperature. Pour over cake; let stand until set.

Makes 12 servings

SWEET POTATO COCONUT BARS

30 vanilla wafers, crushed (see Tip)

1½ cups finely chopped walnuts, toasted,* divided

1 cup sweetened flaked coconut, divided

¼ cup (½ stick) butter, softened

2 cans (15 ounces each) sweet potatoes, well drained and mashed

2 eggs

1 teaspoon ground cinnamon

½ teaspoon ground ginger

¼ teaspoon salt

¼ teaspoon ground cloves

1 can (14 ounces) sweetened condensed milk

1 cup butterscotch chips

To toast walnuts, spread on baking sheet; bake in preheated 350°F oven 6 to 8 minutes or until browned, stirring frequently.

1. Preheat oven to 350°F.

2. For crust, combine vanilla wafers, 1 cup walnuts, ½ cup coconut and butter in medium bowl until well blended. (Mixture will be dry and crumbly.) Press two thirds of crumb mixture into bottom of ungreased 13×9-inch baking pan, pressing down lightly to form even layer.

3. For filling, beat mashed sweet potatoes, eggs, cinnamon, ginger, salt and cloves in large bowl with electric mixer at medium-low speed until well blended. Gradually add condensed milk; beat until well blended. Spread filling evenly over crust. Top with remaining crumb mixture, pressing lightly into sweet potato layer.

4. Bake 25 to 30 minutes or until knife inserted into center comes out clean. Sprinkle with butterscotch chips, remaining ½ cup walnuts and ½ cup coconut. Bake 2 minutes. Cool completely in pan on wire rack. Cover and refrigerate 2 hours before serving.

Makes 2 dozen bars

TIP: Vanilla wafers can be crushed in a food processor or in a large resealable food storage bag with a rolling pin or meat mallet.

APPLE FRITTERS WITH TWO SAUCES

Strawberry Sauce

1 package (12 ounces) frozen unsweetened strawberries, thawed

Butterscotch Sauce

6 tablespoons (¾ stick) butter

¼ cup granulated sugar

¼ cup packed dark brown sugar

⅔ cup whipping cream

1½ tablespoons lemon juice

1 teaspoon vanilla

Apple Fritters

Peanut or vegetable oil for deep frying

1 cup whole milk

¼ cup (½ stick) butter, melted

Grated peel and juice of 1 large orange

1 egg

1 teaspoon vanilla

1 large tart apple, peeled and chopped

3 cups sifted all-purpose flour

½ cup granulated sugar

1 tablespoon baking powder

½ teaspoon salt

Powdered sugar

1. For strawberry sauce, process strawberries in blender until smooth.

2. For butterscotch sauce, melt 6 tablespoons butter in small saucepan over medium-high heat. Add ¼ cup granulated sugar and brown sugar; stir until melted. Add cream; cook and stir 2 minutes. Remove from heat; stir in lemon juice and vanilla.

3. For fritters, heat 2 to 2½ inches oil to 350°F in large saucepan over medium-high heat; adjust heat to maintain temperature.

4. Combine milk, ¼ cup melted butter, orange peel and juice, egg and vanilla in large bowl; mix well. Stir in apple. Combine flour, ½ cup granulated sugar, baking powder and salt in medium bowl; gradually stir into milk mixture until blended. (Batter will be thick.)

5. Drop batter by ¼ cupfuls into hot oil. Fry 3 to 4 fritters at a time 8 to 10 minutes or until evenly browned and crisp, turning frequently. Drain on paper towel-lined plate.

6. Dust fritters with powdered sugar; serve immediately with strawberry and butterscotch sauces for dipping.

Makes 4 servings

SOUTHERN OATMEAL PIE

1 refrigerated pie crust (half of 14-ounce package)

4 eggs

1 cup light corn syrup

½ cup packed brown sugar

6 tablespoons (¾ stick) butter, melted and cooled slightly

1½ teaspoons vanilla

½ teaspoon salt

1 cup quick oats

Whipped cream (optional)

1. Let crust stand at room temperature 15 minutes. Preheat oven to 375°F.

2. Line 9-inch pie plate with crust; flute edge.

3. Whisk eggs in medium bowl. Add corn syrup, brown sugar, butter, vanilla and salt; whisk until well blended. Stir in oats until blended. Pour filling into crust.

4. Bake 35 minutes or until edge is set. Cool on wire rack. Serve warm or at room temperature with whipped cream, if desired.

Makes 8 servings

NEW ORLEANS-STYLE PRALINES

2 cups packed brown sugar

1 cup half-and-half

$\frac{1}{2}$ teaspoon salt

2 tablespoons butter

2 tablespoons bourbon *or*
    1 teaspoon vanilla

1 package (10 ounces) chopped
    pecans (about $2\frac{1}{2}$ cups),
    toasted*

**To toast pecans, cook in large skillet
over medium heat 4 to 6 minutes
or until lightly browned, stirring
frequently.*

1. Line two baking sheets with parchment paper or foil. Combine brown sugar, half-and-half and salt in heavy medium saucepan; cook over medium heat until sugar is dissolved and mixture begins to boil, stirring occasionally.

2. Attach candy thermometer to side of pan, making sure bulb is submerged in sugar mixture but not touching bottom of pan. Continue boiling about 20 minutes or until sugar mixture reaches soft-ball stage (235° to 240°F), stirring occasionally. (Watch carefully; candy will be grainy if overcooked.) Remove from heat; stir in butter and bourbon. Stir in pecans.

3. Working quickly, drop mixture by tablespoonfuls onto prepared baking sheets. (If mixture becomes too thick, stir in 1 to 2 teaspoons hot water and reheat over medium heat.) Cool completely, about 30 minutes. Store in airtight container at room temperature up to 3 days.

Makes about 34 pralines ($1\frac{1}{4}$ pounds)

COCONUT SPICE CAKE

½ cup granulated sugar, plus additional for cake pans

2½ cups all-purpose flour

1½ teaspoons baking powder

¾ teaspoon baking soda

½ teaspoon salt

1½ teaspoons ground cinnamon

¼ teaspoon ground cloves

¼ teaspoon ground nutmeg

¼ teaspoon ground allspice

¼ teaspoon ground cardamom

½ cup (1 stick) butter, softened

½ cup packed brown sugar

4 eggs

1 teaspoon vanilla

1½ cups light cream

¼ cup molasses

1½ cups shredded coconut

Cream Cheese Frosting (page 187

⅔ cup orange marmalade

1. Preheat oven to 350°F. Grease three 8-inch round cake pans; sprinkle with enough granulated sugar to lightly coat bottoms and sides of pans.

2. Combine flour, baking powder, baking soda, salt and spices in medium bowl; mix well. Beat butter in large bowl with electric mixer at medium speed about 2 minutes or until creamy. Add ½ cup granulated sugar and brown sugar; beat 3 minutes or until light and fluffy. Add eggs, one at a time, beating well after each addition. Beat in vanilla.

3. Combine cream and molasses in small bowl. Add flour mixture to butter mixture alternately with molasses mixture, beating well after each addition. Stir in coconut until blended. Pour batter evenly into prepared pans.

4. Bake 20 minutes or until toothpick inserted into centers come out clean. Cool in pans 10 minutes. Loosen edges; remove to wire racks to cool completely.

5. Prepare Cream Cheese Frosting. Spread two cake layers with marmalade; stack on serving plate. Top with third cake layer. Frost top and side of cake; refrigerate until ready to serve. Garnish, if desired.

Makes 12 to 16 servings

CREAM CHEESE FROSTING: Beat 4 ounces softened cream cheese in large bowl with electric mixer at medium speed until creamy. Gradually add 2 cups powdered sugar; beat until light and fluffy. If desired, beat in milk, 1 teaspoon at a time, for thinner consistency.

Chicken (*continued*)
Chicken and Sausage
Jambalaya, 130
Chicken and Waffles with
Sriracha Maple Syrup, 18
Cornish Hens with
Andouille Stuffing, 134
Crispy Ranch Chicken, 85
Hickory-Smoked Barbecue
Chicken Wings, 52
Old-Fashioned Chicken
and Dumplings, 116
Oven Barbecue Chicken,
100
Southern Country Chicken
and Biscuits, 92
Southern-Style Chicken
and Greens, 124
Chicken and Sausage
Jambalaya, 130
Chicken and Waffles with
Sriracha Maple Syrup, 18
Chili Spaghetti Casserole,
106
Chocolate
Double Chocolate Pecan
Brownies, 164
Loaded Banana Bread, 6
Chorizo and Corn Dressing,
152
Citrus Candied Nuts, 40
Classic Deviled Eggs, 34
Classic Macaroni and
Cheese, 137
Coconut
Coconut-Pecan Sweet
Potato Casserole, 156
Coconut Spice Cake, 186
Loaded Banana Bread, 6
Sweet Potato Coconut
Bars, 178
Coconut-Pecan Sweet
Potato Casserole, 156
Coconut Spice Cake, 186

Cola
Cherry Soda Poke Cake,
161
Hickory-Smoked Barbecue
Chicken Wings, 52
Lime Chiffon Pie, 174
Spicy Pork Po' Boys, 86
Collard Greens with Bacon,
138
Cookies & Bars
Double Chocolate Pecan
Brownies, 164
Snickerdoodles, 172
Sweet Potato Coconut
Bars, 178
Corn
Chorizo and Corn
Dressing, 152
Corn Fritters, 42
Deep Bayou Chowder, 59
Fruited Corn Pudding, 146
Stewed Okra and Shrimp,
104
Corn Fritters, 42
Cornish Hens with Andouille
Stuffing, 134
Country Time Macaroni
Salad, 62
Crabmeat
Crab Shack Dip, 36
Southern Crab Cakes, 48
Crab Shack Dip, 36
Cream Cheese Frosting, 187
Creamy Fruit Salad, 76
Crispy Ranch Chicken, 85

D
Deep Bayou Chowder, 59
Dips & Spreads
Crab Shack Dip, 36
Pimiento Cheese, 31
Rémoulade Sauce, 38
Double Chocolate Pecan
Brownies, 164

E
Eggs
Classic Deviled Eggs, 34
Sweet Potato Breakfast
Nests, 28

F
Fish
Cajun Blackened Tuna, 111
Pan-Fried Catfish with
Hush Puppies, 126
Skillet Tilapia with Rice
and Beans, 114
French Dip Sandwiches, 128
Fried Green Tomatoes, 32
Fruited Corn Pudding, 146

G
Garlicky Mustard Greens, 158
Gelatin
Cherry Soda Poke Cake, 161
Lime Chiffon Pie, 174
Strawberry Salad, 60
Greens
Collard Greens with Bacon,
138
Garlicky Mustard Greens,
158
Shrimp Rémoulade Salad,
78
Southern-Style Chicken
and Greens, 124
Sweet and Sour Turnip
Green Salad, 66

H
Ham
Black Bean Soup, 80
Black-Eyed Pea Soup, 64
Country Time Macaroni
Salad, 62
Ham and Cheese Bread
Pudding, 14

189

METRIC CONVERSION CHART

VOLUME MEASUREMENTS (dry)

$\frac{1}{8}$ teaspoon = 0.5 mL
$\frac{1}{4}$ teaspoon = 1 mL
$\frac{1}{2}$ teaspoon = 2 mL
$\frac{3}{4}$ teaspoon = 4 mL
1 teaspoon = 5 mL
1 tablespoon = 15 mL
2 tablespoons = 30 mL
$\frac{1}{4}$ cup = 60 mL
$\frac{1}{3}$ cup = 75 mL
$\frac{1}{2}$ cup = 125 mL
$\frac{2}{3}$ cup = 150 mL
$\frac{3}{4}$ cup = 175 mL
1 cup = 250 mL
2 cups = 1 pint = 500 mL
3 cups = 750 mL
4 cups = 1 quart = 1 L

VOLUME MEASUREMENTS (fluid)

1 fluid ounce (2 tablespoons) = 30 mL
4 fluid ounces ($\frac{1}{2}$ cup) = 125 mL
8 fluid ounces (1 cup) = 250 mL
12 fluid ounces ($1\frac{1}{2}$ cups) = 375 mL
16 fluid ounces (2 cups) = 500 mL

WEIGHTS (mass)

$\frac{1}{2}$ ounce = 15 g
1 ounce = 30 g
3 ounces = 90 g
4 ounces = 120 g
8 ounces = 225 g
10 ounces = 285 g
12 ounces = 360 g
16 ounces = 1 pound = 450 g

DIMENSIONS

$\frac{1}{16}$ inch = 2 mm
$\frac{1}{8}$ inch = 3 mm
$\frac{1}{4}$ inch = 6 mm
$\frac{1}{2}$ inch = 1.5 cm
$\frac{3}{4}$ inch = 2 cm
1 inch = 2.5 cm

OVEN TEMPERATURES

250°F = 120°C
275°F = 140°C
300°F = 150°C
325°F = 160°C
350°F = 180°C
375°F = 190°C
400°F = 200°C
425°F = 220°C
450°F = 230°C

BAKING PAN SIZES

Utensil	Size in Inches/Quarts	Metric Volume	Size in Centimeters
Baking or Cake Pan (square or rectangular)	8×8×2	2 L	20×20×5
	9×9×2	2.5 L	23×23×5
	12×8×2	3 L	30×20×5
	13×9×2	3.5 L	33×23×5
Loaf Pan	8×4×3	1.5 L	20×10×7
	9×5×3	2 L	23×13×7
Round Layer Cake Pan	8×1½	1.2 L	20×4
	9×1½	1.5 L	23×4
Pie Plate	8×1¼	750 mL	20×3
	9×1¼	1 L	23×3
Baking Dish or Casserole	1 quart	1 L	—
	1½ quart	1.5 L	—
	2 quart	2 L	—